Daughters Forever, Sons Forever
By Linda Kracht

First Edition

www.FortifyingFamiliesofFaith.com

Book and Cover Design By:
Traditions Communications LLC
17272 605th Avenue
Janesville, MN 56048
www.TraditionsCommunications.com

Printed in the United States of America.

International Standard Book Number
ISBN: 978-0-9818741-0-4

Library of Congress Control Number: 2008931117

Daughters Forever, Sons Forever

By Linda Kracht

Contents

Acknowledgements

While I began this book several years ago, it seems like yesterday in many ways. It is made possible by the generous support of many people.

First, I have to thank my husband, Dave, and our children, who believed I could do this. They sacrificed much while I worked on this book. I can still hear in my mind Kyra's frequent, sweet query: *How's the book, Mom*? Thank you Dave, Kelly, Patrick and Kyra. Our older children, while no longer living at home, have also been extremely complimentary and supportive. Thank you Ryan, Michelle, Lindsay and Michael.

Secondly, I wish to thank my editor, Jacqueline Nasseff Hilgert. This is our second book together and I know that neither would be what they are without her expertise, wisdom, encouragement, direction, and counsel.

Thanks to Joan Czaia, my friend and illustrator, who has worked on projects with me for quite a few years, volunteering hours without complaint; Joan is just a godly woman with whom I enjoy working.

Thanks to the Society of St. Gianna for lending her image to this book.

Thanks to Daphne Buckingham and her daughter, Glenys, and to Jim Benyon and his son, Sam, for lending their images for use in this book.

I wish to thank all the mothers and fathers who attended or worked with me for the past eleven years when I put on *Daughters Forever, Sons Forever* workshops at St. Agnes Catholic School in St. Paul, Minnesota. Some parents suggested taping the program, others recommended a text to accompany the program, so here it is.

I wish to remember the late Msgr. Richard Schuler who first allowed me to put on this program; he trusted me enough to "experiment" with this project. It has grown better through the years of his encouragement. May God grant him eternal rest and may we someday meet again.

Finally, I wish to remember my parents, brothers and sisters, who have supported and loved me, and are a part of who I am. Thank you Mom, Kathy, Karla, Kevin, Gloria, Dan and Brandon. May God grant eternal peace and rest to you, Dad. We miss you.

Introduction

Most parents want to pass along their faith and offer their children the fruits of their experiences. They want to offer their children wholesome, value-centered information on many topics, including human sexuality. After all, the responsibility for teaching children about sex lies with parents. For some, though, facing up to this responsibility becomes a challenge. Strong parents realize they must debunk societal myths that permeate our super-sexed American culture but they don't know where to turn for resources they can trust. Some parents shy away from the subject because it makes them self-conscious; still others find themselves beleaguered by the barrage of sexually explicit images thrown at them from the media or others, so they give up. When our children hear false messages about sex from television, movies, magazines and music, they desperately need their parents to launch a values-based counter offensive rooted in truth.

Sadly, some parents today feel their words have no impact so they allow their voices to fall silent. In this situation, silence is not golden. There are groups that operate with a distinctive voice and they are not silent when it comes to sex education. Planned Parenthood has adopted a mission and vision for the sole purpose of "getting to our kids." Hollywood and other "elite" chip away at our families every day with their psychosexual babble. There is money to be made from the destruction of our children's values and parents must remain vigilant to protect the future of our society.

Parents can't sit idle while pretending their children know it all when what they know about themselves and others is really very limited by lack of experience and knowledge. Parents everywhere need to shoulder the responsibility that society would prefer they ignore. Parents are the primary teachers for their children and few lessons will impact children's lives more than when they learn what God has planned for them and their lives including control and knowledge of their bodies.

Parents *cannot* really claim primary responsibility for their children's formation when they allow others to teach their children about human sexuality and other important matters. This book is meant to provide you with resources, knowledge and the courage and conviction to teach your children about human sexuality. I am not a moral theologian, physician, or family counselor. My credentials include being a wife, a proud parent of seven children, a very proud grandparent of seven (and counting), and an experienced teacher of natural family planning for the Couple to Couple League. I do not pretend to be the expert; for that I draw on "experts" to support my arguments. However, I also believe when it comes to your children, you are the expert. You are the most qualified person to pass along to your teen your family's philosophies and knowledge about human sexuality, for these lessons are personal and best discussed within the family. You have the opportunity to pass on to your children both your experience and what those lessons taught you in hindsight. Even things you learned the hard way – by figuring things out as you went along – contain practical and theoretical knowledge. It's good to arm that knowledge with true conviction.

A few years ago, I was invited to address a group of mothers and daughters attending an "All in God's Plan" program. My topic was natural family planning. Not long into the program the girls, some as young as age ten, began fidgeting. It was the classic sign of disinterest in a subject matter of no immediate relevance to their state in life. Many hadn't yet experienced ovulation or menstruation and thus had no practical knowledge of how they would soon change physiologically, psychologically and practically.

They didn't know what the heck I was talking about!

I had two pre-teen daughters who I had tried to interest in the science of the female reproductive system and they too responded with lackluster enthusiasm. It was at that point when several ideas struck me.

First, these girls weren't interested in this information about sexuality and human-person biology at this time simply because it was over their head. This detailed of information wasn't immediately needed because it didn't jibe with or coincide with what they were actually experiencing. They couldn't relate or even pretend to be interested. Sometimes a concept is too complicated to understand so it's easier to just accept as it is or dismiss it.

Secondly, I was astounded to see that many of the mothers in the group appeared to be hearing much of this information for the very first time. I realized few had ever attended natural family planning classes, such as ones offered by the Couple to Couple League, in which details of the physiology of the human person are demystified.

Finally, I discovered that we all have a real need to first understand the biological person in order to better respect our bodies and thereby make appropriate decisions.

So my question became, at what age should we present information on human sexuality to children? I had to recall my pre-menstrual youth for an answer. I remember seeing a film in my Catholic grade school about how babies formed in the womb. Not much of it made sense to me at the time and I remember my friends and I talking about it afterwards, all of us befuddled with the exception of one girl who shocked us when she announced that sperm comes from your dad and your mom has the egg and they have sex and that is how the babies are made. "No way, not my mom and dad!" was my inner response.

I remember thinking I could get pregnant from a sperm if I used the toilet too soon after my father or my brothers. As far as sex, I had no idea what that meant; it had never entered my consciousness because of my age and innocence. As ridiculous as my misunderstanding sounds today, at the time, it nearly became a phobia. I honestly felt, at age eleven, I was probably pregnant and boy-oh-boy did I worry! I would push on my belly hoping to expel the pregnancy even though that action conjured up feelings of guilt. (Even at that young age, I understood that pregnancy equals baby and pushing out pregnancy equaled pushing out baby.) This crazed thinking of mine went on for some time until I finally realized that my stomach wasn't getting bigger so I must not be pregnant. Perhaps, I finally began to have a clearer understanding of pregnancy because my sisters and I talked about this film a lot!

My point is this: rather than bringing a certain "joy" which follows truth and knowledge, too much information delivered at the wrong time can result in misunderstanding, confusion – even fear. Parents, I caution you not to disturb the dormancy of innocence. I worry whether similar confusion results from the Drug Awareness Resistance Education (DARE) programs taught to many of the nation's fifth graders. Sexuality and drug education is inappropriate when it is ill timed and may do more harm than good. As a result, I stopped teaching young girls about things that they might easily misunderstand or misconstrue and I caution all parents to consider their child's maturity level before examining certain topics.

Daughters Forever, Sons Forever attempts to bring together both short long term purposes. In the short run, I hope to provide you with information which can best be described as a human sexuality (health) curriculum and information with an emphasis on developing character and virtue. Long term I hope it helps you connect with your teen so together you navigate the road ahead. Furthermore, I hope you imagine yourselves as you were destined to be His daughter or His son, forever. In his children's book, *Love You Forever*, Robert Munsch writes: "I'll love you forever / I'll like you for always / as long as I'm living / my baby you'll be."

So it is for all parents. We all want the best for our children; the information in this book is meant to help you and your children learn and grow together.

In the following chapters you'll find information culled from a variety of sources, including talks presented during my *Daughters Forever, Sons Forever* program. Please enjoy, learn and grow from the information gathered herein. In the back of the book there is a list of resources I recommend to supplement the information compiled here.

You live your life as witness to your children. The information your children hunger for is frequently more personal than technical in nature, despite what secular institutions might want you to believe. The material presented in this book is a resource for you — a starting point. But what children need most is parental guidance that flows from the heart to the soul. Trust yourself to be the teacher God calls you to be. And may God bless you and your daughter or your son as together you discuss God's plan for them in and through their bodies. ❦

Daughters Forever, Sons Forever

By Linda Kracht

chapter one

Opening a Dialogue

Recall those Polaroid cameras that allowed our photographs to develop right before our eyes. If the photo was taken at the right exposure, meaning the light was just right, within a few seconds of emerging from the camera, figures would begin to appear on the photo. Sure, the earliest image didn't have vibrant color or the optimum contrast; this came much later. But, given the right amount of time combined with ideal conditions, eventually a fully developed, rich photograph was the result of our picture taking. We also got the thrill of watching it all unfold before our eyes.

It's the same way when we communicate with our children. We give them the right amount of "light" by setting a good example and communicating our values to them and then slowly, over time, they become well-balanced, fully developed adults – the type of person society badly needs. And we get to watch this development happen right before our eyes. What a joy! What a responsibility!

As parents, the primary responsibility to give children the time, nurturing and influence they need to fully develop into God's image is primarily ours alone. Communication is the means by which we pass along to our children our values and beliefs. This means our verbal messages, our non-verbal cues and the examples we set take on the same importance to our children's development as light, chemicals and time impact the development of a photograph.

Without light, photography couldn't exist. Without your diligent guidance, a child cannot grow to adulthood centered in God. How and what you communicate to children will determine if they receive the light they need to develop properly.

Avoid the lecture

Want to send your teen running for the door? Start talking to them about how different life is today from when you grew up or how much worse you had it when you were a kid. Then add the story about how you had to walk twenty miles to school every day through blinding snowfall.

I expect they might respond by asking: "Were police patrolling your schoolyards? Were there crack dealers prowling the halls of your school? Were there sexual predators posing as teenagers back then, like they do now on our internet chat sites?"

I grew up in the 1950s, a time when family life appeared stable, marriages appeared solid, and gender roles were clearly defined. Family life included many children and although most people lived plainly, the 1950s are often referred to as a "golden era." I'd be willing to bet most people who lived during this era would agree there has been a general decline in moral values and public stability in the decades since and generally we are weaker as a society now.

Is this assessment true? Not according to author Stephanie Coontz.

In her book, *The Way We Never Were*, Coontz purports that the good life of the 1950s included anxieties over the Cold War. There was a lot of hiding going on. People pretended not to be unfaithful in marriage; people pretended they weren't homosexual. Spousal abuse wasn't considered criminal behavior. Rape and incest victims were dismissed as victims of a subconscious oedipal desire.

Coontz offers additional statistics from the time: Between one fourth and one third of all marriages that began during the decade of the 1950s ended in divorce; more than two million legally married couples lived apart from each other; and the number of marriages entered into due to a teenage pregnancy more than doubled.

There were also economic challenges. "A full 25 percent of Americans, forty million to fifty million people, were poor in the mid-1950s, and in the absence of food stamps and housing programs, this poverty was searing," Coontz writes. This was the part of life in the 1950s in which I have first-hand knowledge.

Neither of my parents finished high school. After they married, my father converted an old chicken coop into a three-room house in which they raised me and several other siblings. They eventually expanded this chicken coop into a three bedroom, one bathroom house (no basement) for the family which grew to include seven children. This was in Dickinson, North Dakota.

The 1950s is a decade filled with fond memories of childhood, says author Linda Kracht, pictured here in 1954. Above center are the author's parents, Jean and Charles Krank, on their wedding day in 1949.

When I was young my parents had two of us kids sharing a spare bed in their "master" bedroom while two of my sisters shared a tired old sofa-bed in the living room. I remember walking to school to the beat of loose soles flapping against the pavement. All of our clothes were handmade and by the time my clothes reached me, they'd already seen several years of wear from my sisters. Believe me, there was nothing remotely fashionable about what I wore to school!

We didn't have an indoor toilet until my sister, who was eighteen months older than me, nearly fell down the hole in our outhouse. She was rescued in the nick of time by my distraught, hard-working mother.

For my parents, the 1950s were rough times. I, on the other hand, look fondly on my childhood years as a happy period when material possessions didn't matter – only my parents' love and guidance did.

Comparisons between decades or generations too easily become generalizations which develop into myths. They don't capture the full scope of the positives and negatives of each time. And who can prove us wrong or right about comparisons with certainty? People forget bad times. They move on. They change. Often, even siblings raised in the same household remember events differently.

Comparing the ways of old with today, even through statistics, can't possibly reveal any deep truths about peoples' beliefs. Memory, perspective and experience all skew with age; nearly all people at one point or another will take creative license with their personal history. Suffice it to say, there never will be a true golden age until we reach Heaven.

It's far better to focus our attention on forward thinking, praying and acting. We can't control what happened before us; we cannot change the past. We *can* and *must* prepare our children for a better future by giving them the tools to make wise and careful choices for their lives. The degree to which society's morals have degenerated from the time of your own childhood is irrelevant; it shouldn't become a dwelling place for you. The fact is there are people you can influence, witness to, help, teach, and model what it means to be made in the image and likeness of God. Statistics mean little when it comes to your daughters or sons, your nieces or nephews. Help them turn away from choices that are unhealthy, life threatening, and immoral.

"I urge you therefore, brothers, by the mercies of God, to offer your bodies as a living sacrifice, holy and pleasing to God, your spiritual worship. Do not conform yourself to this age but be transformed by the renewal of your mind, that you may discern what is the will of God, what is good and pleasing and perfect." Romans, 12:1-2

Be an authentically Catholic parent

My experience with the Couple to Couple League has taught me that in order to teach what a gift natural family planning is to married couples, I must use it and model it with success and joy. The same holds true when teaching children to live virtuous lives. In order to effectively convince teenagers to embrace chastity, parents must not only talk the chastity talk, they must walk the chastity walk. This means parents joyfully ascribe to the teachings of the Catholic Church in areas of moral and spiritual matters even if they are intricate (without gaining deeper insight) or controversial (to those cynical to Truth). Truth is self evident to faithful believers and can become self evident also to anyone searching for it through study, reflection and prayer. Today's controversial moral issues often revolve around *Humanae Vitae* or *Theology of the Body,* the Church's teaching on our bodies, families and marriage, which address contraception, divorce, artificial reproduction and homosexuality. You will find explanations to why these are offensive to our nature in subsequent chapters.

Families will not live in tranquility if there are serious and obvious contradictions of beliefs within the family unit. The same holds true for our society. When various cultural or religious groups hold opposing views they often co-mingle while attempting to "convert" the other. This conversion may be subtle, via social pressure, or more overt as through politically-motivated incentives. The Catholic Church has not been immune to this sort of in-fighting or attempts by some to modify doctrine to fit certain lifestyle choices.

Many Catholics don't agree with the moral teachings of the Church yet continue to call themselves Catholic; considering the "empty pew syndrome" plaguing many parishes, I wonder how many of these people have just stopped going to Mass. The sad fact is millions identify themselves as Catholic even while they stray from Catholic teachings. When children realize their parents are picking and choosing what to believe according to their personal taste – they'll believe this approach is also right for them. This is NOT authentic Catholic parenting.

Yes, there are many Catholic parents who hold strong opinions about morality that are contrary to Church beliefs. Yet they hold onto these opinions without evaluating them or calling them into question through serious debate, research or investigation. Dr. Janet Smith, noted Church theologian, recently commented that she isn't interested in hearing the opinions of people who haven't given more than five minutes of thought before forming them.

One cannot reasonably expect teenagers to reject the lure of internet porn, the intrigue of "hooking up," the desire to dress provocatively, or the false belief that pre-marital and casual sex is okay as long as it's "safe," if your son or daughter sees you choose similar "adult-themed" lures within your marriage or hears you bad-mouthing Church doctrine and/or moral teachings. Authentic Catholic parenting is based on living as a personal witness to the love of Christ as he teaches us through His Church. Our teenagers ought to be taught that the Ten Commandments are merely God's way of helping us to live without regrets. Your teenagers are savvy; they will see through phony sentiment and turn a deaf ear to any lessons not rooted in honest, truthful living.

If you want truth in the world to prevail, start by infusing God's truth in your children. God's moral code is black and white. The good news is that we don't have to figure all these issues out for ourselves; the Church is there to help us along the way.

Some parents worry that they just don't know when and how to start the dialogue. This text and accompanying workbooks should help with these decisions. Other parents wonder how much to say and when to have those all important talks. Use your parental instincts; test the occasion in your children by watching for responses, cues, questions and understanding.

Some parents worry that their own past mistakes preclude them from "coming down" on their children in those same areas. Some parents assume since they made it through mistakes, their children will do so also. While it is true that mistakes can help forge stronger character if we learn from them, it is also true that some mistakes have dire, life-threatening consequences that time cannot erase. If we can help prevent our teens from making similar mistakes, aren't we helping them get to adulthood safely, securely and without baggage or regret?

If you believe that God's Truth is expressed in the Church's moral and spiritual teachings, shoulder your parental responsibilities and pass this faith and these values onto to your children. You are capable, with His help, to carry out this mission. Your job should naturally include trying to improve the lives of those around you — including your teens.

You won't have to prove that God is right — He does that. You just need to be the faithful servant and witness. Be encouraging. Press on despite any wedges others may try to insert between you and your teen. Muster the courage to shove aside those wedges and begin the dialogue; connect with your teen for both your benefits. ❦

chapter two

Landmines for Teens

When you live your life according to the example set by Christ and raise your children to do the same, it quickly becomes apparent how each day you must shelter your family against the prevailing winds of a decaying culture. Consider polls that suggest the majority of Americans favor abortion rights or gay marriage. Have you ever wondered, as I have, if a poll suggesting the opposite would find its way into the newspaper?

As children grow toward adulthood they begin to exercise their independence. As they do, they will encounter facets of our culture intended to lure them away from God; I call them landmines and they include: peer pressure, materialism, immodesty, popular music, television, the internet, pornography, and the latest dangerous fad called "hooking up."

When you brought your innocent babies to church for their Baptism, you vowed to raise them to believe in God (Father and Creator), Jesus Christ (His Son and our Savior), the Holy Spirit and the *holy* Catholic Church and to reject Satan and all his evil ways. You vowed to reject deceit and corruption – the same explosives that lie in the path of innocent children, adolescents and teens, placed there by a corrupt society more invested in *creating* things that destroy core family foundations and beliefs. How must you respond? First, make your home a fortification that shields your children from these things that lead them toward harm. Then, march its perimeter much like a soldier charged with protecting a compound. Like a soldier, you need to learn about the enemy in order to provide effective security. You need to stay alert. You must march against profanity with vigilance, hope and faith.

Teach your children to turn their backs to the temptations prevalent in today's society and walk with a loving and just God. Instruct your children in ways that help them to develop a strong, moral inner core. Using your own lives as guideposts, teach your children about sacrificial love, Christ's courage and the rewards (i.e., peace, joy) that await them as they successfully shun the profane ideas that permeate the culture.

Indeed, a culture war exists in America and you and your family must push forward – under constant assault – to maintain the values you hold dear. That's not always easy, especially when assaults become personal; you may at times be incorrectly labeled intolerant, right wing, conservative, or rigid, simply because you hold fast to God's truth. But hold fast you must, for the sake of your children.

Children require parental advice and good counsel long past the point when they reach the age of reason. In fact, research conducted recently reveals that the "brain's frontal lobe which allows a person to think in abstract, prioritize thoughts, anticipate consequences, and plan and control impulses is not fully developed in teens. This part of the brain undergoes the most maturation during adolescence and is the last part to develop completely ... this part of the brain isn't completely developed until the early twenties," according to psychologists.[1]

Furthermore, while our children's brain is under "construction" during adolescence and teen years, parents have a great opportunity to influence and be important to their maturing child. Psychologists know that as the frontal lobes "mature so does the quality of thinking. Teenagers don't think more so much as they think better. They become capable of understanding symbolism, thinking abstractly and appreciating a more sophisticated sense of humor."[2]

Further fine tuning allows teens to communicate better, remember more information, think more logically, evaluate problems better and choose more appropriate solutions than when they were younger. However, as their brain undergoes development, not everything works the way we parents might hope and expect. For instance, disorganization and poor decision making are part and parcel of transitioning from a younger brain to an adult brain. Therefore, parents are key to helping their teens avoid big mistakes during this developmental period.

While adults frequently rely on the brain's frontal lobe to make decisions and think logically, teens rely on the emotional center of the brain to interpret the same information. Remember their frontal lobe is still in flux. This means that teens tend to respond more emotionally to parents, friends, stimuli, information and suggestions. While accelerated teenage brain development allows for an ease of learning new things, it poses some risks to them as well. Teens are at the greatest risk at this time of their lives for developing addictions; this is discussed more later in the chapter.

What is peer pressure?

We all benefit from some peer pressure in our lives. Positive peer pressure helps hold us accountable for our thoughts, words and actions. In many cases, it's what keeps us from doing things that might make friends think twice about "hanging" with us; it also keeps us from actions that might damage our reputation or prevent a company from hiring us. In other words, peer pressure can be a positive force that gives us incentive to stay on track — track defined as learning how to live out God's plan for our lives.

Wouldn't it be great if we all behaved and thought and acted as God does? But, we are human beings with sinful tendencies. Fortunately, He loves us permanently and unconditionally. He constantly pours out Himself to us by means of grace. He also gives others to us to lend an example of how to live. This is why the lives of the saints are important; they provide us with real examples of persons who lived out the faith in an excellent way. The saints are a great source of positive influence and we should strive to imitate them.

Of course, peer pressure can also become a negative influence, especially when it drives a wedge between a child and his or her parent, or a child and God, or between parents. Negative peer pressure chips away at core beliefs; often, it connects our children to superficial, negative influences. James Stenson in his guide for parents entitled *Preparing for Peer Pressure* writes: "Peer pressures are only permanently successful when they move into a vacuum in the children's inner character. The peer pressure problem, therefore, is not one of merely avoiding 'bad companions.' That's virtually impossible these days. The key question really is: Why is a child attracted irresistibly to such companions in the first place?"

We know some children give in to more negative peer pressures than others. The key difference, Stenson asserts, can be found in the character of the child. "A well-formed conscience, a firm religious belief, a prayerful relationship with God, a trust in his parents' powers of judgment, a lifetime habit of self-control (saying no to one's feelings), a respect for the rights of others – all these traits firm up a young person's will to resist," he writes.

Parents who ignore their responsibility to teach their children the pillars of strong character leave their precious children vulnerable to the damaging effects of negative peer pressure. Character isn't inherited, after all; it's developed under the careful, loving but firm guidance of parents who themselves courageously face negative influences. Developing character is like filling an empty cup — pour in the right ingredients and its taste will be authentic. Likewise, a cup that remains full, will less easily be refilled with the wrong ingredient(s). An empty cup or even a half empty cup, by contrast, begs for a refill; when a wrong ingredient is added, the taste is degraded.

Sheryl Feinstein in her book *Parenting the Teenage Brain,* tells us that peer influence is strongest with regard to music, clothing and curfews. Parents' influence remains strongest over spiritual beliefs, morals and politics, when provided consistently.

Another facet of negative peer pressure could be termed "group think." How many teenagers, when faced with decisions about how to dress, choose to imitate the image and likeness of Britney Spears or Snoop Dog? It takes a strong individual to respond to the interior call of the conscience and choose differently than a Top 40 music artist or friends. Without a well-developed inner conscience (self core), a vacuum can form. Teenagers look for guidance from parents but if it isn't offered freely, concretely and lovingly they look elsewhere — friends or even the pop culture — for answers. Today, group think helps glamorize *conspicuous consumption,* which all too often leads to a complete disregard for social justice. Rather than acting as an individual concerned about the well being of others, group thinkers make decisions based upon how they might best gain the acceptance of others. With group thinkers, the quest for acceptance leads to consumerism, service to self, popularity contests, and to the accumulation of goods that increasingly fail to satisfy the emptiness in the soul that cries out for purpose.

Even those who tout diversity are often hard-pressed to think or act independently of one another. Group think may not allow members to consider how their words and actions affect those who won't, or are unable to, advance their agenda. Some of these groups ignore the voice of the most vulnerable among us: the unborn, the aged and the infirm.

Negative peer pressure is not just a landmine for teenagers. All of us are tempted by it's lure. Who doesn't fall prey to flashy magazine headlines, covers, and advertisements that tout the latest fashions or feature trendsetters? A small child who wants his sibling's toy will pull it away, sometimes quite agressively. By doing this, he is already saying he wants what his sibling has. Parents should discourage this emerging "group think."

Rick Warren in the *Purpose Driven Life*, writes: "Many people are driven by the need for approval. They allow the expectations of parents or spouses or children or teachers or friends to control their lives. Others are driven by peer pressure, always worried by what others might think. Unfortunately, those who follow the crowd usually get lost in it."

Warren also writes that while he can't name all the keys to success, he's sure one key to failure is the attempt to please everyone. "Being controlled by the opinions of others is a guaranteed way to miss God's purposes for your life," he said.

"No one can serve two masters. He will either hate one and love the other, or be devoted to one and despise the other. You cannot serve God and mammon." (Matthew, 6:24)

God took very bold measures when He needed to teach early believers that He was the Creator of all life on earth while also the final judge of Heaven. While being both perfectly loving and perfectly just, He cannot tolerate evil because it is incompatible with His goodness. It's true He gave us a completely free will because of His unconditional love for us, it's also evident there are forces in the world out to trip up this free will. That's because evil exists with the sole purpose of leading us away from God. We abet evil when we believe Heaven and Hell are too far away to worry about.

As parents, we have an obligation to form our children's character long before problems develop. But first, we need to practice or model virtue ourselves. In order to be more perfect models to our children and help them spurn negative influences, our actions and words must be in sync with our beliefs and values. Here are some ways to become a positive model to teens:

• Stand firm when children ask for things or want to participate in activities which you don't approve. Parenting is not a means by which you seek acceptance and popularity from your children.

• Monitor your family's spending habits. Be aware of how you spend: do you model restraint or recklessness when consuming goods and services? Are your purchases based on need or desires? Are you wasteful? Do you over-emphasize style, name brands or fashion? Your children will become consumers in your mold.

• Promote community service and become active in your Church community. Demonstrate the desire to continue growing in your faith by attending faith formation classes as a family and as a couple. Family time spent serving others will reap greater rewards than time spent at the mall.

• Help your children become critical thinkers by encouraging them to question the messages behind advertising, peer advice, movies, and other mass media. Talk to them about the "business" of selling and how peoples' emotions can be manipulated through wordplay.

• Teachings of the Catholic Church on God, morality, sexuality, sin, evil and final judgment are healthy peer pressure. Here's what the *Catechism of the Catholic Church* says: "God created man a rational being, conferring on him the dignity of a person who can initiate and control his own actions. God willed that man should be left in the hand of his own counsel,' so that he might of his own accord seek his Creator and freely attain his full and blessed perfection by cleaving to him." (Chp. 1730) Furthermore, we seek out our Creator as we seek to better understand and conform ourselves to the Church's teachings.

In the Old Testament God used severe punishments to prove the seriousness of sin. We live long past these days and are blessed to have a Church to help us understand the seriousness of sin and its consequences. It also offers us the gift of the sacraments which impart grace and enable us to experience true freedom as we desire it. The question then becomes, do we want the opportunity to live life to its fullest or do we think "that's something I'll save for tomorrow?" Furthermore, do we expect our children to figure it out tomorrow or do we want to give them a head start on this opportunity?

The "almighty" dollar

We probably all want to believe we are not materialistic. But are we? Do we hesitate to examine our lifestyles? Do we make excuses for purchases and consumption excesses? Take a look at your credit card bill. Perhaps you have more than one.

I hear people complain they have less money per month to spare even though they earn far more than when they first married. Could this be because they now define themselves by what they own, what they wear, where they work out and which school their children attend? As American parents, we rush our children from one after-school activity to another; combine soccer clinics, birthday parties and piano lessons with dinner on the run and more activities in the evening. It's no wonder parents spend without thinking and never think about saving. Who even has the time to think? But what lessons do we teach our children as we rush them around town to "acquire" more and more experiences or even the necessary items participation in extra-curricular activities require?

I remember when our older children received money on their birthday and at Christmas from their grandparents. We always put that money into their bank accounts to teach them the importance of saving for the future – a time when they'd need something like college funds, etc.. I admit I've done my younger children a disservice because I've allowed them to spend these monetary gifts on things they *desire* rather than encouraging them to become savers. It gets worse. I've even given them money and let them figure out their own gifts! When I examine my own behavior, I realize my actions were not just wrong but harmful because they promoted materialistic desires in my youngsters.

Encourage children to become savers rather than consumers by providing for their needs and helping them discern the difference between "needs" and "wants."

Believe me, my children don't *need* anything. But they *want* things! By giving them money to spend as they please, I actually fueled their desire to acquire and consume things they clearly can live without. Wouldn't it have built better character had I encouraged them to give part of that money to charity instead of spending it on themselves? Or, to have taught them to delay their gratification and save until they actually need something?

I encourage all parents (myself included) to get serious about teaching children to respect money before it begins to wield power over them. Children – all of us, really — are bombarded daily with messages to buy this, buy that, buy whatever! Ironically, marketers use the word "save" in order to spur us to spend. You've heard the campaigns: "You can have it now (even if you can't afford it) if you buy it on credit...no payments for three years!"

By never having to wait to accumulate, children miss out on the opportunity to practice self-discipline. A child who insists he must have the hottest new toy puts his parent in the difficult position of having to teach restraint while also practicing it. But is there a lesson more important for your child to master than the lesson of self-control? When a parent indulges an eight-year-old child in what seems an innocent desire – a new toy – the message conveyed to the child is that desires need attention and waiting has no value. Think this scenario forward ten years to a son on the cusp of adulthood; it's not inconceivable to think that after a decade of being indulged in simple desires, a young man may not be able to wait until marriage before indulging sexual desires.

One guest speaker at a *Sons Forever* event mentions in his talk "When I Was Your Age," how he saved all the credit card applications mailed to his house in his son's name. After one year, he showed us what he'd collected. The applications filled an entire fifty-five gallon trash bag, and they all had come in addressed to one person – his minor son! (This talk is available online at www.FortifyingFamiliesofFaith.com.) Think about how this mountain of paper could lure your teenager into a see-it, want-it, I'll-buy-it-on-credit mindset. How quickly could your child become enslaved to a credit card company? Remember, spend-versus-save decisions will develop into habits.

Consumerism causes us to cower when another credit card bill arrives and behave like Pavlov's dog salivating (in our case spending) every time the bell rings (we see the newest gadget). We worry we are missing some grand opportunity if we don't get one more credit card or buy another pile of stuff. We thus become enslaved and don't even realize it.

Juliet Schor, author of *The Overspent American*, writes that throughout the 1980s and 1990s, middle class Americans acquired at a greater rate than any previous generation. "By the mid nineties, America was decidedly anxious. Many households felt pessimistic, deprived or stuck, apparently more concerned with what they could not afford than with what they already had. Asked what constitutes 'the good life,' people in 1991 focused far more on material goods and luxuries than they did in 1975. Items more likely to be part of the good life now than then include a vacation home, a swimming pool, a color TV, a second color TV, travel abroad, nice clothes, a car, a second car, a home of one's own, a job that pays much more than the average, and a lot more money. Less likely, or no more likely, to yield the good life, according to respondents, were a happy marriage, one or more children, an interesting job, and a job that contributes to the welfare of society."

It's hard to read those words and *not* conclude that materialism and consumerism have contributed to the decline of both family and community life! As a people of faith, we sometimes fare no better. We all see or know Catholic families who choose larger houses and fancier cars over having babies or saving troubled marriages – all in the pursuit of self interest. Would it be such a disadvantage for a child to grow up in a home without a Jacuzzi or a fancy car? When people believe it's better to have fewer children than to strap the few they have with less, they feed the values crisis plaguing America. As conscientious as we think we are, almost without realizing it, we become absorbed into the culture that consumes and what gets used up in the process is not the goods and services we buy but our belief that we are on earth to serve a higher power – God.

Can we continue to hold onto the belief that marriage and children are the bedrock of society when we read survey results such as the one above? When we believe that what we buy is more important than what we can naturally create through marriage, society suffers. When we prefer disposable objects over immortality, society decays.

Children add freshness to our world. G.K. Chesterton reminds us in, *The Well and the Shallows,* that: "children are a very sign and sacrament of personal freedom. He is a creation and a contributor. This child is the creative contribution of the parents to creation. Furthermore, he is much more beautiful, wonderful, amusing and astonishing than any stale stories, jingling jazz tunes, or 'priceless' products turned out by machines."

I recall my college years when life's needs seemed simple. I wanted to finish my education, find a spouse, settle down and have children. If I was lucky, my spouse and I would be able to buy a home. Today we see college educated young people often push aside commitment as they practice marriage by living together, then replace their first live-in with another and another; some trade in their first spouse in pursuit of a second and sometimes even a third. They acquire a home where they park several cars then set out to acquire all the conveniences and toys of modern life. They delay childbearing which often makes it difficult for them to naturally conceive. And yet, the pursuit for more continues. Yet, as Schor asserts, "most Americans would deny that by their spending they are seeking status in the usual meaning of the word — looking to position themselves in the higher economic stratum ... What stands out about much of the recent spate of spending is its *defensive* character. Parents worry because their children need computers and degrees from good colleges to avoid being left behind in a global economy.

"Not surprising, as upscale competitive consumption intensified, family finances deteriorated," Schor writes. "Sixty-three percent of those households earning incomes between $50,000 and $100,000 per year are now in credit card debt."

Children learn consumption in the home earlier than ever. Even a kindergartener recognizes brand names and can equate a certain model of car with an assumption about its owner. Through marketing ploys and questionable parental behavior, children begin to believe that the "haves" of the world have greater intelligence, success, education and control in their lives than the "have nots." When you make a purchase – especially one for your child – ask yourself how that purchase reflects you or feeds your own desires. Could you be living vicariously through your child as you spend more and acquire things that improve your child's status? After all, how many children really ask for all that they receive?

Written centuries ago, the ninth and tenth Commandments seem particularly relevant to our twenty-first century struggle with consumerism: "Thou shall not covet your neighbor's wife," and "Though shall not covet your neighbor's possessions." When you try to align your life with God's plans and Commandments, His Church and His Word, it's much easier to resist the lure of reckless spending. But before you can help your children learn how thoughtless spending can ensnare them and degrade their values, you must analyze your own actions when faced with desires versus true needs. Consider the steps below as you teach your children that money is a tool to be used for good, not for evil. After all, contentment is found in Christ; you won't find it on sale at the mall!

• When you face purchasing decisions select a durable product over a disposable one. People tend to develop emotional attachments to durable goods, making it less likely they'll want to replace it unnecessarily.

• Stand firm when your children pressure you to buy them unnecessary things. Remember, it is your job to teach children how to turn away from negative influences – even when that makes you the "bad guy." Giving in to the desire for instant gratification, either yours or your child's, eventually paves the way to dangerous consequences whereas parental lessons in self-control will pay dividends long after your child leaves home.

• Never practice the old adage: Do as I say, not as I do.

• Become a resourceful borrower/lender. Share resources with friends and relatives instead of acquiring duplicates of things you use occasionally.

• Frequent those wonderful community resources such as parks and libraries.

• De-commercialize gift-giving occasions – especially Christmas! Start new traditions in your family that circulate around the meaning found in Christ's birth, life and death. Our children happily recall our homemade Jesse Tree, the advent wreath lightings, special holiday meals including the lengthy Seder meal on Holy Thursday. The ability to recall specific gifts pales in comparison to the memories of "sacred" family traditions.

• Warn your children about the risk of buying on credit. They must learn that purchases can end up costing two, three and sometimes four times the advertised price when factoring in interest and late payments. Also, show them how some credit card companies entice customers with initial low rates then switch them to higher rates after a few months or once they make a late payment.

• Show older children how a family budget works. Children need to learn the relationship between a paycheck and monthly obligations; they also need to learn why saving is important. Children need to see you model charitable giving. The goal should be to raise children who have healthy attitudes toward money. You don't want your child to become covetous, and self-indulgent; you also don't want a child to grow miserly or stingy.

• Teach children Juliet Schor's definition of the opportunity cost of employment. When you work more, you certainly earn more, but you also have less time for family activities and recreation. Talk about how employment outside the home also means increased transportation, clothing and meal costs. Is spending time away from the family to earn money for "things" in the best interests of your family? The answer will differ for each of you, but your children, as they mature, need to see the trade offs in terms of lost family time and increased stress.

• Limit – or eliminate – television. Juliet Schor presents evidence in her book that a link exists between watching television and increased family debt. She argues that television escalates people's appetite for consumption. People want what they see. Furthermore, television marketers have become increasingly brazen as they use sexually-charged images to catch our attention even when selling items as seemingly innocuous as deodorant. Today's parents may not catch or know how to effectively counter, such messages. I believe it's much easier to just hit the off button and seek out healthy entertainment for your family such as playing games, reading together, camping, gardening, cooking, exercising, or doing volunteer work together.

By encouraging children to fight consumerism and materialism, you also help them battle the desire to conform that springs from peer pressure. Money is an important tool in everybody's life. Used recklessly, however, money accelerates the decline of our values and dooms us to an unfulfilling diet of empty calories. Free yourselves from the see-it, want-it, do-whatever-it-takes-to-get-it, mind set. By trusting that God provides, money can be viewed as a useful tool to be used judiciously.

Dressing for success

What does dressing for success mean? Does modesty play a part in dressing for success? The answer varies from family to family. I think some people would prefer girls wear dresses that reach the floor with sleeves that cover their arms all the way to their wrists. These same parents might choose an all-out ban on girls dressed in swimsuits or slacks. Others, meanwhile, don't think about modesty relative to how a teenager dresses and won't admit there are implications for a girl who bares her cleavage to the world or a boy whose pants nearly fall off his backside. I believe somewhere in between, there's a workable compromise for adolescents who may view themselves as stars on the world's stage, and their parents who don't want their children to become a distracting star on that stage. (I only wish I could convince the people who stock our clothing stores of this!)

Social researchers tell us that clothing plays a role in peer acceptance by forming first impressions, allowing for positive or negative feelings about self, and allowing for expression of one's individuality or desire to conform. Clothing is readily seen by others. Most assume that a person's attire is of their own choosing. Because of this, clothing serves as a means by which we judge gender, age, social status, occupation, personality, interests and values, behavioral expectations and group membership, says Leslie Davis in *Clothing and Human Behavior, a Review*.[3] Clothing also stimulates behavioral responses in observers, whether they be at school, work, or during recreation such as on dates or at parties. In other words, clothes matter.

Clothing is the means by which others judge our age, gender, social status, occupation, personality, interests and values.

Allow me to tell you a story of what happened to me one day as I took my children shopping for shoes. My youngest son Patrick was no longer nursing at the time but his breastfeeding experience wasn't too far behind him. That day, we were assisted by a sales girl who was wearing a very low-cut top; I swear it was *three* sizes too small. I can still recall Patrick's look of astonishment as this clerk nearly revealed her set of "milkies" to my young son as she laced up his shoes. The clerk seemed oblivious to Patrick's locked stare (perhaps he was recalling happier moments spent breastfeeding) but I was embarrassed by it – and upset that this young girl seemed oblivious to my son's astonishment.

Since that encounter, girls' fashions haven't improved. Today, it's common to see girls wearing negligee-like tops and undergarments as outerwear, and at very young ages!

Modest attire is a way to protect our children, boys and girls, so they may achieve success while at work, play, or at school. Yet fashion is linked to the social process. While it's true that fashion choices are rooted, in small part, by a need for personal expression, they also communicate sexual selection, availability, and sexual attractiveness. One's choice of attire becomes a significant non-verbal cue that signals availability and attraction to the opposite sex. After a woman marries, she typically discards sexier "singles" clothing because they become unnecessary; she's now found her mate.

In his book *The Decline of Males*, Lionel Tiger writes: "Centuries ago, women accepted societal norms that dictated standards of dress, including modesty. Standards for modesty have fluctuated along with styles and definitions of sexual attractiveness. More recently, clothing standards have been influenced by a new phenomenon, which interjects a higher sexual component into fashion — the development of the birth control pill."[4] Tiger continues with the following: "In the 1960s women were subject to new forms of fashion and demeanor. They escalated the sex game. Rather suddenly there emerged a stunning array of candidly erotic and voluptuous novelties such as the abandonment of bras, the shortening of skirts, the popularity of tight jeans, and even the astonishing topless fashions at various resorts." Well, there's a way to get a man's attention (i.e. Patrick and the shoe salesgirl)!

Tiger makes an interesting observation, one that has basis in science. There are naturally occurring hormones that impact the interplay between the sexes and these hormones are altered when birth control pills are used by women. I find it telling that women have become more explicit in how they express their sexuality through their clothing choices as they've ingested chemicals, which diminish the effect of natural hormones that had previously done this work for them.

The increased sexuality of today's clothing is readily observable. We see varying degrees of exposed breasts and buttocks with emphasis of different body parts and eroticisms worked into clothing on display at schools, the workplace, and everywhere in between, from TV stars to news reporters. Fortunately, conservative clothing ideals rooted in faith or based on age and ethnicity also exist. We need not be solely dependent on cultural ideals as we choose to dress ourselves and our children.

When we allow fashion designers to set the mark for appropriate attire, we lose important influence over our children's opinions – and their choices. Again, it's necessary to take a stand against those whose seek to undermine our values for material gain. Don't throw up your hands and despair that there's nothing suitable for purchase in the stores. There is! It just requires more perseverance from you. Here are other ways you can promote modesty in your teenagers' clothing choices:

• As parents, define modest dress for your household. Model it and pass it on to your children. Teach your daughter what skirt/dress length and apparel size best flatters her figure without being too tight, or too revealing. She can look perfectly wonderful and simultaneously modest under your guidance. Teach your son about modest dress as well.

• Help your daughter recognize, and steer clear from, clothing that enhances her erotic appeal rather than her innocent appeal. This is an area where fathers can be particularly helpful. Dad, you should lavish your daughter with praise and attention when she is dressed beautifully and appropriately and explain what certain clothes do to the male imagination.

• Check your own clothing choices. Do you aim to influence by how you dress? Do your clothing choices reflect a healthy modesty?

• Teach that clothing makes a statement about yourself. Dress for success modestly and encourage your teen to do the same. If modesty is lost through clothing choices, it may be lost in other areas as well.

• Set your family's standard for what's acceptable attire and enforce those standards consistently – for boys and girls.

Furthermore, adolescents who work or are given liberal allowances or gifts become participants in the marketplace. Having spending money gives adolescents power to make personal purchases that align with their own tastes or the collective tastes of their peer group. A teen who asserts this power can leave parents feeling "left out" of some very important decisions.

Lack of parental influence during purchasing allows others to influence a teenager's choices. Sociologists inform us that as adolescents undergo puberty and psycho-social changes, they experience insecurity relative to who and what they are and how they should present themselves to the world. This is why parental influence is so important.

During adolescence, females tend to be more dissatisfied with their bodies than males; girls, more than boys, use clothing to boost self-image. Girls also have a higher desire to feel and look attractive compared with boys. Receiving positive reinforcement from family is therefore extremely important. Fathers, in particular, need to convey love and appreciation for their daughters *as they are*.

Boys, more than girls, tend to conform to their peers regarding clothing; they like to wear clothes that give them an appearance of strength. This explains why boys will emulate a favorite athlete by wearing his jersey.

Teen Poverty in America (Fig. 2-1)

We just spent several hours observing teenagers hanging out at our local mall. We came to the conclusion many teenagers in America are living in poverty. Most young men we observed didn't even own a belt; there was not one among the whole group.

But that wasn't the sad part. Many were wearing their daddy's jeans. Some jeans were so big and baggy they hung low on their hips, exposing their underwear. I know some must have been ashamed their daddy was short because their jeans hardly went below their knees. They weren't even their daddy's good jeans, for most had holes ripped in the knees and a dirty look to them.

It grieved us, in a modern, affluent society like America; there are those who can't afford a decent pair of jeans. I was thinking about asking my Church to start a jeans drive for "poor kids at the mall." Then on Christmas Eve, we could go Christmas caroling and distribute jeans to these poor teenagers.

But here is the saddest part...it was the girls they were hanging out with that disturbed us the most. Never, in all our lives, have we seen such poverty-stricken girls. These girls had the opposite problem of the guys. They all had to wear their little sister's clothes. Their jeans were about five sizes too small! I don't know how they could get them on, let alone button them up. Their jeans barely went over the hip bones. Most also had on their little sister's top; it hardly covered their midsections. Oh, they were trying to hold their heads up with pride, but it was a sad sight to see these almost grown women wearing children's clothes.

However, it was their underwear that bothered us most. They, like the boys, because of improper fitting of their clothes, they had their underwear exposed. We had never seen anything like it. It looked like their underwear was only held together by a single piece of string.

We know it saddens your heart to receive this report on the condition of our American teenagers. While we go to bed every night with a closet full of clothes nearby, there are millions of "mall girls" who barely have enough material to keep it together. We think their "poorness" is why these two groups gather at the mall; boys with their short daddies' ripped jeans and girls wearing their younger sisters' clothes. The mall is one place where they can find acceptance. So, next time you are at the mall, doing your shopping, and you pass by some of these poor teenagers, would you say a prayer for them? Will you pray the guys' pants won't fall down and the girls' strings won't break?

Parents who are interested in ensuring their children develop into godly young people must provide them with a well-rounded education — even in areas such as technology.

Family, friends and other people influence one's perceptions of self. Having a well-developed core helps one maintain a positive self image. As an adolescent's image of self develops, strong family bonds help him remain resilient against negative pressure from outside influences. Parents must not relinquish their duties and responsibilities for children's formation to fashion designers, peers and store clerks.

On a lighter note, one of my daughters sent me the commentary in Figure 2-1, on the state of our nation's youth – in terms of their attire. I hope you enjoy it as much as I did.

Pop culture on the air

Have you heard the phrase, "He who sings, prays twice?" It's from St. Augustine and it always comes to mind when I hear great music from the past. Mozart, Bach and Beethoven all opened their souls to create great works and this is the reason their music resonates centuries after they've passed. If you compare their work to what is generated by the pop artists of today, the longevity of this appeal seems all the more significant. But there I go waxing nostalgic again!

What worries me about today's music is not the duration of its potential appeal. What concerns me is the content of some music, the lyrics and their sometimes subtle, oftentimes overt messages of hopelessness, destructiveness and despair that hits our children's ears and chips away at their innocence. I am also concerned that adolescents don't know the benefits of quiet time, a time for reflection. How can they? When are they without earphones blaring, damaging both their hearing and their awareness of the world around them?

When I listen to modern music lyrics I hear "cool" defined through behaviors that are selfish, arrogant, defiant, lawless, and promiscuous. Some of the most popular artists are self-described "bad boys" and "bad girls" who only evoke "bad attitude." Plenty of songs cross the airwaves today to promote hatred and violence. Too many songs encourage: disrespect toward women, racism, the use of illegal drugs, cheating or lying, and the glorification of other destructive behaviors. These songs should concern you because they launch a direct assault on decency, civility and virtue. The people who create and promote these types of songs are preying — not praying!

Although it may be difficult, try to make a point to listen to a few of these songs. You'll quickly discover how vile these lyrics are – and dangerous, even to the casual listener. Think about how these messages may damage a young psyche when they are repeated over and over and over. Our children are still learning about their world and haven't yet developed effective filtering devices when facing such extreme profanity.

Consider carefully this information before making any gift purchases for music or music accessories, which enable your adolescent to listen to songs out of your earshot. Consider also the consequences of not knowing which songs they're accessing.

In *The O'Reilly Factor for Kids*, Bill O'Reilly writes that any song that glorifies destructive behavior is dangerous. I agree. These adolescents belong to your child's peer group. So don't let your child become obsessed with this, or any form of entertainment. Pay attention to what your children are listening to. If it's music that encourages them to despair or disrespect others – help them now by turning it off!

Music and language express and influence our emotions. We listen to certain songs generally because they make us feel good or they communicate feelings or moods to which we can relate. Consider how technicians use music in movies to induce fear, happiness, sadness and other emotions. Even marketers use music to sell products. Researchers have found that increased exposure to hard rock and heavy metal music with lyrics is positively associated with more frequent negative behaviors among its listeners.[5] Furthermore they found that lyrics enhanced the emotions conveyed by sad or angry music. This means that lyrics affect mood and behavior – it isn't a benign addition to music.

The popularity of a song or an artist is particularly troublesome for parents if the artist or music is offensive in nature (violent, sexualized, disrespectful, anti-authority and promoting drugs or alcohol). Popularity of a song drives its listener to want to understand what everyone else seems to know; it motivates the listener to discover the meaning of the words. Eventually a listener will discover the meaning of lyrics from peers, watching movie videos, or through personal knowledge or experience.

Finally, the influence of both lyrics and music is very real on the listener. Studies show that while certain young people with particular views may be especially attracted to a particular kind of music, all young people are vulnerable to the influence of the lyrics in the music they listen to.[6] Music and lyrics do affect listeners.

All together, music influences and motivates listeners to understand the attitude of the music particularly when it's very popular. This influence is what motivated the Parent Teacher Association and the Parents Music Resource Center (PMRC), which was started in 1985 by Tipper Gore, Susan Baker and two other women, to urge parents to get involved in all music purchases. Clearly, music affects our young people's attitudes.

Some parents have tried to create a music rating system thinking it would be helpful. The practicality of such a rating system raises questions, such as: Who would rate the music? Whose moral compass would assess the music product? Whose *interpretation* of the lyrics would be used for the ratings? Furthermore, some hip-hop artists claim the PMRC's rating efforts are a boon to sales of their albums or hit songs. They claim getting on the PMRC's list nearly guarantees that their songs or albums will be bought by defiant children.

When it comes to shielding children from offensive music and lyrics, parents need to be vigilant on their own.

Music videos

Music videos compound the problems presented by offensive music. While lyrics may carry multiple interpretations, music videos assign a song a visual meaning. Research has demonstrated that young adolescents often are unable to correctly interpret the lyrics of a song due to their age, life experience and immaturity. Music videos solve that dilemma by interpreting the lyrics for the viewer/listener.[7]

Like television, music videos limit "creative" interpretations of song lyrics; nothing is left to the imagination. Once a song's "music video images" are embedded in a youth's head, a simple replaying of the song on the radio or their iPod conjures up images of the music video rather than other possible interpretations, including the original intent of the songwriter when it differs from the music video.

Though music videos are generally short and have poorly developed story lines, their powerful imagery can promote themes such as sexualized beauty, status, money and power. Studies have proven that adolescents who watch music videos frequently over-estimate real-life sexual behavior. These same adolescents also showed strong approval or acceptance of the following negative behaviors: premarital sex, sexual harassment, and adversarial sexual relationships, stereotypical images of powerful, virile men and sexually objectified women, and teen dating violence. The younger the music video viewer, the more likely he or she will accept and endorse music video stereotypes.[8]

Popular culture on the tube

Television long ago abandoned its innocent beginnings and now could be considered a dark alley which you'd be wise not to send your children into unsupervised.

Too many parents don't heed this warning, however. Approximately 25 percent of American children watch between four-and-a-half and eleven-and-a-half hours of television each day. The average number of television hours viewed daily is three-to-four hours per day up from two-to-three hours in 1970. How is this possible? What are they watching? Furthermore, the average American child spends roughly six-and-a-half hours every day using the following media outlets: television, movies, video games, computers and the internet.[9] Children spend four times as much time watching television as doing homework.

Television's early developers promised us that TV would bring American families together. In its infancy, the harshest criticism launched at the medium was that it often lulled people into a state of mindlessness. People watched television for its entertainment value and over time have become more passive and less resistant about the programs they watch and less concerned about how long they watch. Some forty years after first being introduced, television separates family members; in many households, each person has a television set so everybody can enjoy their own favorite program while the others in the home enjoy theirs.

Few would argue that TV content brings families together either. Few programs are suitable for the entire family including the advertisements that interrupt the programming. Often used as a babysitter, television is a very poor substitute. Studies show that heavy use among the young interferes with reading and language development. Heavy viewers have lower academic achievement, hold onto more cultural stereotypes, and spend less time practicing, acquiring and learning social skills. They also spend fewer hours playing challenging, imaginative games.

Some studies show that certain children also become desensitized to violence as a result of their viewing habits.

Other studies show that reading, writing, doing math, practicing musical instruments, and/or participating in sports actually contributes to the buildup or development of the adolescent and teen brain, whereas passive activities like television watching does not.

Besides, important practice time for reading, writing, and doing mathematics is lost when children sit in front of the television. Some studies show children's writing styles often mimic sitcom conversation: fragmented and illogical. Heavy television viewing is also being blamed for the increasing weight problems among adolescents. Inactivity aside, television viewers frequently snack and drink sugar-laden beverages while spending time in front of the tube.

The method by which television producers entertain America has changed too. Sophisticated movement, constant movement and pattern changes on the television screen combined with brilliant colors, sound effects and sharp graphics grab hold of viewer's attention.[10]

Sex is now the prevalent theme found on television, injected into the medium under the guise of entertainment. This is a problematic influence over our young people because a number of studies, including one conducted by the American Pediatric Society, demonstrate that television captivates teens while influencing their sexual attitudes, values and beliefs.

If the mainstream media were to be believed, inappropriate sexual activity occurs in America with great frequency. Dr. Stephen Genuis and Shelagh Genuis include in their book, *Teen Sex Reality Check*, these frightening statistics: "In the 1999/2000 television season, nearly 70 percent of all shows on television portrayed sexual content, with one out of every ten shows depicting or strongly implying sexual intercourse. The vast majority of these encounters involved unmarried couples and the percentage of teen characters involved in acts of intercourse had tripled from two years before. Only a small amount of these programs included any reference to the potential negative outcomes of these sexual encounters."

It gets worse. According to *Sex on Television and Its Impact on American Youth*, sexual content was found in 64 percent of all 2001-2002 television programming. The content included talking about sex (61 percent of programs), overt portrayals of sex (32 percent of programs), and implied portrayals of sex (14 percent of programs). Only 15 percent of the 2001-2002 programming season included references to the risks associated with sex outside marriage, such as pregnancy or sexually transmitted diseases. Furthermore, 3 percent of the sexually active characters, on television during the 2001-2002 season, were teenagers.

Parents can't sit idle while television twists their children's attitudes about sex and simultaneously offers a dangerously skewed version of reality and consequences related to sexual activity. Remember, television viewing already comes with the added risk of numbing our critical thinking skills as it conditions us to relax, accept what we see and be entertained.

Adolescents are savvy; they use available media sources to assess what's going on in the culture and to discern what's hip and what's not. Their observations influence their behavior — this is known as social learning. Being exposed to sexuality on television, and in movies and videos, hastens adolescent initiation of sex. Unfortunately, hastening doesn't mitigate regret. A recent national survey revealed that nearly 66 percent of teens wish they had waited longer before initiating sex.[11]

Like other pursuits, your choices in television programs should reflect the values you hope to pass along to your children. We all enjoy humor when it is appropriate but we also know we need to say no when television shows exceed the boundaries for wholesome, family-style material. When we opt to fills our minds with anti-family images, thoughts, situations, and decisions that do *not* reflect the image and likeness of God but are more suited to a godless view of entertainment or reality, we become part of the culture of death rather than the culture of life.

You've heard the story about the frog that is placed in a pot of cold water then set over a low flame. The frog will swim happily in the pot as the water gradually warms not realizing it's in danger until it's too late and then it's cooked! It's the same way for our children. Help your children be entertained by images that reflect godly values so that they won't become just like the unsuspecting frog, and get cooked too!

Television will never be an acceptable substitute for parental attention, especially today as programs incorporate more and more sexual innuendo and violence. With television and radio, it's imperative you remain a vigilant monitor for the songs your children listen to and the programs your children watch. With all entertainment, television, radio, movies, music videos, and even video games, get involved with your children as they peruse the options available and be absolutely certain that your family's values and ideals are supported by what they watch and listen to. Other ideas regarding media entertainment include:

• Help your children avoid getting swept up in hype. Tell your children it's okay to like music but not just because every other teen likes it. Older children need to make up their own minds about their music (with guidance) and that means they should be required to defend their choices to you in mature terms.

• Help your children expand their musical horizons. Expose them to live concerts held in parks, at a local university or as part of heritage festival.

• Encourage your children to get musical at home by providing them with real instruments and lessons. And, always encourage them to sing in church.

• Keep entertainment systems in family shared spaces rather than in private spaces such as bedrooms.

• Share your family's television rules with the parents of your children's friends and ask that those rules be respected while your children visit.

• Even "family" television shows often incorporate zippy one-liners that are inappropriate when they challenge the lines of authority between parent and child. Be cognizant of the danger that lurks behind "wit" when humor comes at another's expense.

• Television commercials are often laced with images of sex and violence, and these commercials oftentimes appear during the breaks of "family" shows. This is just one more reason to look beyond the television set for family-style entertainment.

• Restrict media usage in the home to no more than several hours per day and limit activity to certain hours and certain places in the home.

• Limit the channels that come into your home.

• Determine whether your children turn on the television or computer the instant they enter the home. If so, this could be a tell-tale sign of a problem.

• Continually assess whether your child would rather watch television, play computer games or surf the internet to any other activity. Again, this may signal an over-dependence on electronic media for entertainment.

• Award television viewing only after first reading books, doing homework, and playing imaginative games. Create a point system to be used for these awards. There was an entertaining Berenstein Bear's children's book entitled *Too Much TV* – it creatively discussed how the family lost interest in many fun family activities after getting a new television. The tale relates how mother and father bear limited television time to recapture the love of the outdoors, crafts, etc. This book holds real life lessons and is worth reading to young children.

• Consider using token-activated meters on your home electronic equipment. One such device, by Stokes Corporation, is called Token TV. You can find out more information about this token meter from their web site: www.tokentv.com.

The internet: A treasure trove and a danger

The internet provides opportunity and landmines for adolescents *and* adults. While most parents old enough to have teenagers at home have had to adapt to the advent of computer technology, teenagers simply take the resource for granted. After all, in their lifetimes, computers have always existed. They use it for homework, gaming, chatting, shopping, research and more.

While internet use is a worldwide phenomenon, North America has the most penetrated market; we have more than 237 million users representing about 71 percent of the entire population, adults and children. The next heaviest user region is Oceania/Australia boasting 57 percent penetration. The worldwide use of the internet has reached at least a 19 percent penetration level and it's increasing as you read this.

People use the internet for a variety of reasons, as seen in figure 2-2.

Face it. Your children are more comfortable than you when it comes to using a computer. Teenagers especially seem to be able to navigate through the online environment without fear and often, because of this boldness, they will either stumble onto sites with content inappropriate for them or they may go looking for the sensational. Because of a technology-driven role reversal (in many homes it's the teenager who holds the expertise in computer use while parents just muddle through) very little instruction is given on how to safely navigate cyberspace. Without being instructed on safe online communication, teenagers risk putting themselves in harm's way.

From the familiar surroundings of your family's living room or home office, teenagers can get lulled into a false sense of security as they enter chat rooms with the innocent intention of merely socializing. Teenagers who begin corresponding with strangers may inadvertently reveal their identity or location; or they may do so purposely in an effort to connect with people they've met online. The accelerated intimacy and lack of inhibition within online chat rooms lends itself to young people being at risk for exploitation. With youth so highly engaged in electronic communication, it's crucial you learn to whom and what your teenager connects.

The internet provides educational benefits to students as well. The internet allows them access to online journals, expert opinions and research, data, homework supports, discussion boards which help foster learning and positive peer teaching if properly directed and monitored. Furthermore, it allows them to fine-tune their computer expertise.

New sites which encourage teenagers to meet new people and share personal information have emerged in recent years to increase the challenges for parents as they fight to protect their children's safety. One study, found online at www.gov-tech.com/gt/print-article.php/id, reported that 62 percent of students in the fifth through the eight grades use the internet to meet new people. They shared the following information:

- Twelve percent shared their first name with their new friend.
- Three percent revealed their last name.
- Thirteen percent shared their gender.
- Seven percent shared their age.
- Two percent shared their phone number.
- One percent shared their home address.
- Eleven percent said they arranged to meet this new friend in person.

Fig. 2-2:
How we use the Internet

Content: news, people, companies, industry, computer, medical, products,educational purposes.
Format: journals, books, patents, standards, legislation, regulations, databases, data sheets, figures, reports, discussion groups
Source: vendors, government, organizations, academic institutions, commercial, global, internal.
Nature: print, people
Graphics and multimedia
Buying and selling

Source: 3M Library & Information Services

MySpace.com, popular among the high school set, and Facebook.com, originally designed for college students, both have soared in popularity since being introduced. The danger of using these sites is real. Children willing to reveal information about their lives and interests to strangers may be lured by the sensationalism of what they see and read in peers files. They also can be enticed to reveal information about themselves that is immodest. There is a time and place for people to open their hearts, bodies and souls to another. That time comes with marriage after having spent many months developing a healthy, non-sexualized relationship.

Teenagers need to be taught to reject the idea of "revealing" themselves in the public square – both in how they dress *and* what they tell – because they don't know who is looking. Sure, it could be just a friend from school reading your child's MySpace web page, but it also could be a potential employer looking for a reason to reject your teen's job application, a lender looking to reject a young adult's loan application, or a criminal looking to cause harm. On the flip side of that coin, teenagers who are naturally trusting will encounter information about others that cannot be verified. Someone who purports himself to be a sixteen-year-old boy may in fact be a middle-aged sexual addict on the prowl who entices your trusting teen into an online revelation in order to launch an attack.

Social networking tools are a perfect starting point for investigators; both for criminal investigators and journalists. Facebook, Technorati, Flickr, YouTube, and MySpace open the door for these investigators and others; it gives strangers access to names, addresses, friends, cell phone numbers, interests, hobbies, photographs, and political affiliations that normally would have been much harder to obtain the old fashioned way — by talking to people or going door to door. Facebook does allow a private site, however, once it's opened to certain groups, it's open!

Young people are putting their lives up for scrutiny in a sometimes unfriendly world. They are posting snapshots of themselves – is this really what they want others to think about them? While enabling some friends to keep in touch the easy way, with a click of a button, it also allows the spread of old-fashioned gossip the new-fashioned way. Again, be wary of how your child uses his or her time with these social networking sites.

Internet porn is an insidious threat to our teenagers, powered by the AAA engine of evil: accessibility, affordability and anonymity. The danger is real and should frighten parents, especially in light of Canadian research that revealed: a majority of teenagers older than twelve have visited adult-only chat rooms; one-fourth of survey respondents have received pornography from someone they met online; the same number indicated that an online acquaintance tried to arrange a personal meeting with them; and, 15 percent actually made personal contact with someone they met in cyberspace. More surprisingly, the majority of adolescents who participated in the study conducted by researchers at the University of Alberta, Edmonton, reported that their parents do not regulate use of the Internet, are unaware of what is being viewed online and do not know who their offspring are communicating with in cyberspace.

As an underscore to this troubling research, I watched a news report on teenagers and the Internet and was shocked to hear that sexual predators went online to connect to children as young as twelve or thirteen and continued their pursuit even after learning police were conducting sting operations in order to catch them. Some of these sexual predators, it was later revealed, held well-regarded jobs in society such as doctors, teachers, preachers, and even military personnel. Still, they risked losing it all in their attempt to lure children into their sordid world.

Some good news emerges from this cesspool of information about porn and adolescents. Children were less likely to be exposed to unwanted sexual solicitation in 2005 (13 percent) than in 2000 (19 percent). Children's solicitation from perpetrators who attempt to contact them still hovers around 3 percent to 4 percent, according to a study reported in *Internet Safety Gone Wild*.[12]

Tell-tale characteristics have emerged about adolescents most likely to access on-line pornography. Adolescents most likely to expose themselves to explicit material on the Internet are: male sensation seekers; dissatisfied with family and personal life; depressed; have accessed sexual content from other media sources; have a fast internet connection, and reached puberty earlier than peers.

Parents need to be aware of when their children reach puberty. Too often, parents dismiss their son or daughter as being too young to discuss sexual matters when, in fact, their children are gripped by curiosity. Any attempt by your child to search for answers in the wrong places needs to be intercepted.

Parents need to remain vigilant about the possible use of the internet or any media for securing sexual images by their adolescent. Research reported in *Cyberpsychology and Behavior* indicates children who view internet porn are more likely to be reported for delinquent behavior, abuse of drugs or alcohol, and need intervention for depression or inadequate emotional bonding.

There are steps you can and should take regarding your Internet access, including firewalls and filters that are widely available and affordable. Seek out advice from your local computer company in order to protect your children. Also consider these steps:

- Have the computer moved out of the child's bedroom and place it in a family room or another room if it is connected to the Internet. Communal places in the home help parents to more easily monitor the sites children visit and assess how long they surf the net.
- Check the history in your Internet browser to see what sites have been visited recently. If the history option is set to clear daily, that's a red flag that your child might be browsing inappropriate web pages.
- Parents interested in ensuring their children develop into godly young people must provide them with a well-rounded education – even in areas such as technology where they might not feel comfortable. Seek expert help when necessary and review Chapters 2222-2223 in the *Catechism of the Catholic Church* for support.
- Explain to your children that images and words which compromise or degrade others, threaten human society.
- Teach children to avoid communication with people they don't know. Several other safety standards to impress upon your children are: never instant message people whose names they don't recognize, change their screen or user name immediately when they feel they are being stalked online. Better yet, consider not allowing any access to chat rooms and instant messaging.
- Teach and learn internet safety. Safety filters are not enough.
- Encourage children, teenagers and young adults that a proper response to an online sexual solicitation is no response at all. Also, they should disclose or report such encounters to you or other people in authority at their schools or workplaces. Report online sexual solicitations to the cyber-tip line of the National Center for Missing and Exploited Children: www.cybertipline.com.
- Teach your children what information they can and cannot give out. The Big Six No's include: No real names; No telephone numbers; No addresses; No school name; No passwords, and No personal information about friends.
- Teach your child to beware of the risks of online social networking.

• Learn the privacy settings on social networking sites.

• Decide if you will allow your teen to visit social network sites. When you allow this, set limits to the amount of time your teen is allowed to use sites such as MySpace.com or Facebook.com.

• Learn tell-tale behavior of predators; teens should know how to warn or block those who make them feel threatened.

• Teens should know that they must extract themselves from any and all uncomfortable situations.

• Teach your child that many people of the same name may be on sites such as MySpace as well as entries set up by people pretending to be someone else.

• Parents should pre-determine what Internet usage is appropriate for which age children. Social networking seems far less age appropriate for ten to fifteen year olds than college-age children.

• Negatives of heavy internet use among our young people include: reinforces shyness in person-to-person contact, internet surfing takes up valuable time, and it reinforces writing skills that are short, choppy and impersonal.

• Filtering, blocking and monitoring software includes: CyberPatrol, NetNanny, and IPrism.

Pornography: the societal scourge

We hear time and again that as long as "something" is done in the privacy of one's home, "something" should not be society's concern. In other words, if it doesn't affect me, it's none of my business; private acts don't negatively affect others simply because they're private acts. This logic can be quantified as "Enlightenment Philosophy" and Americans have fully endorsed this faulty thinking – especially in their support for pornography!

The philosophy of the Enlightenment, which emerged and grew in acceptance during the early twentieth century, purported that humans were rational beings and thus able, because of self-interest, to direct their actions toward civic virtue without coercion by civic or religious authorities. Protestant influences on private judgment affecting individual conscience also shored up the belief that people are basically caring individuals who will presume the best in everybody and will put their efforts toward the betterment of society.

I don't wish to argue for first believing the worst about everyone. However, I believe the Protestant approach that elevates private judgment to a position of authority has led Americans down a dangerous path to the point where our pursuit of "privacy rights" has forced us to accept actions that not only degrade society, but are morally reprehensible, i.e., abortion and pornography.

Consider how pornography is considered by many to be harmless. It generally involves only one person who acts in private so it cannot affect others, the argument goes. However, books have been written and seminars conducted that show pornography does indeed harm society. Numerous times, rapists and murderers have pointed to the use of pornography as the impetus that moved them to violence. It's almost as if they're admitting, the "devil made them do it." Yet, society continues to allow pornography and protects pornographers under the Constitutional Amendment that guarantees free speech. Privacy, it seems, trumps all other rights. Too bad our right to be free *from* profane expression is not equally regarded by the government.

Decades ago, people had to be sly in their pursuit of pornography. Some traveled to other towns for their illicit purchases while others ventured into unmarked buildings in seedy neighborhoods only to emerge later with a purchase wrapped in plain brown paper. Public scorn for pornography was a prime example of positive peer pressure subduing negative behavior.

About ten years ago, I had a close encounter with pornography that I will never forget. My children and I went to a video store to rent a movie for our Friday night entertainment. The children had been excited to come along and as we wandered up and down the aisles, I spied another section in the store I thought we'd missed. We all bounded toward that section, rounding the corner with very innocent eyes to find ourselves under immediate assault from adult-only images pasted on scores of videos. I quickly rustled the children out the door and we've never returned to the store that did nothing to keep innocent eyes from stumbling onto these degrading images.

Today, this type of porn can be delivered right into the privacy of peoples' homes via the Internet or cable/satellite television. People no longer need to sneak around and risk being publicly shamed as they pursue gratification through pornography. As a result, the shock value attributed to pornography decreases while acceptance of its use increases.

So what is the harm of pornography usage? For one thing, "it's become the leading factor in divorce," states Jonathan Daugherty, founder of Be

Broken Ministries in San Antonio.

In her book *Pornified*, Pamela Paul includes comments by California psychotherapist Tina Tessina who points to pornography as a problem for 25 percent of the couples she sees in her counseling practice. "It [pornography] keeps men from dealing with problems that exist in their marriages," Tessina states. "It's avoidance."

"Researchers have found that prolonged exposure to pornography fosters male sentiments *against* having a family at all. For those who already have a family, the urge is to withdraw," writes Paul. Couples are being torn apart because pornography leads to selfish sex, jealous sex, competitive sex, lack of trust and ultimately, cheating.

Furthermore, repeated pornography use can lead to addiction in the same fashion as other mind-altering drugs. Sex addicts have described their reaction to the effects of pornography using terms such as euphoria, high, excitement, and thrill. In *A Male Grief: Notes on Pornography and Addiction*, David Mura writes: "In pornographic perception, the addict experiences a type of vertigo, a fearful exhilaration, a moment when all the addict's ties to the outside world do indeed seem to be cut or numbed. That sense of endless falling, that rush, is what the addict seeks..." The addict – any addict – becomes powerless to the effect of the "addict's rush."

Through this example, it's clear to see that pornography isn't a harmless activity conducted in the safety and privacy of somebody's home. Pornography can be just as dangerous – just as addictive – as heroin, cocaine or crack, all illegal substances.

Steve Wood, founder of the men's ministry "Covenant Keepers," says a drug dealer once told him he had a much tougher time kicking a pornography habit than the drug habit he had in his twenties.

When children are exposed to pornography, their developing sexuality is affected and the younger they are when exposed, and the more explicit their exposure, the more damaging are pornography's effects on them.[13] One unhealthy outcome of viewing pornography is habitual masturbation. (A discussion about masturbation is contained in the *Sons Forever Father's Workbook.*) *Playboy* magazine, unfortunately the periodical of choice for many men and young boys, contains highly-idealized images of women, with which real women cannot – and should not be forced to – compete. Boys who become obsessed with pornography don't learn to connect sex to a relationship with a real woman. This becomes a major disconnect for them, that left unchecked, conditions young men to seek out arousal through imagery instead of through intimacy with a woman.

And don't believe that only non-Christians seek out pornography. A survey conducted in 2000 of clergy members by *Christianity Today* and *Leadership* magazines found that 40 percent of clergy admitted to visiting sexually explicit web sites.

Thankfully, other research hints that our young people understand there are negative implications from using pornography. A 2001 Kaiser Family Foundation survey of fifteen-year-olds to twenty-four-year-olds revealed 59 percent of them thought seeing pornography on line encouraged young people to have sex before they were ready while 49 percent said they believed Internet pornography could lead to addiction and promoted bad attitudes toward women. In a 2002 Gallup poll of teenagers aged thirteen to seventeen, 69 percent of boys and 86 percent of girls said they would feel guilt over surfing pornography on the Internet. With so many young people cognizant of the harmful effects of pornography in terms of skewed perceptions toward women, I am hopeful that careful parenting will protect the innocence of the next generation from the societal scourge that is pornography.

Sex was never designed to be a spectator sport. Sex is the ultimate act by which a husband and wife express the meaning and fullness of their love – a covenant with God that is open to His will. By reading Pope John Paul II's *Theology of the Body,* it's clear we are commanded to love and respect each other as beings crafted in the image and likeness of God. Parents need to study this theology and teach it to their children.

Parents can turn to the moral authority – the Church – for guidelines on how to instruct their children to communicate marital love because society will push Enlightenment philosophies at them and encourage them to believe that what matters most in their lives is privacy. (See Chapter Six for fuller examination of how privacy activism led to legalized abortion.)

Now, more than ever, parents need to take an active role in educating their children about their sexuality and the true meaning of love. Parents must show their kids how true love nurtures our life and our relationship with God. This will give them the fortitude to turn away from dangerous, addictive scourges such as pornography. Young men and young women need to learn how to relate to each other in a healthy sphere of influence offered by solicitous parents and a proactive church community. Here are other things to consider:

- Using steps outlined in the Internet section above, parents can shield

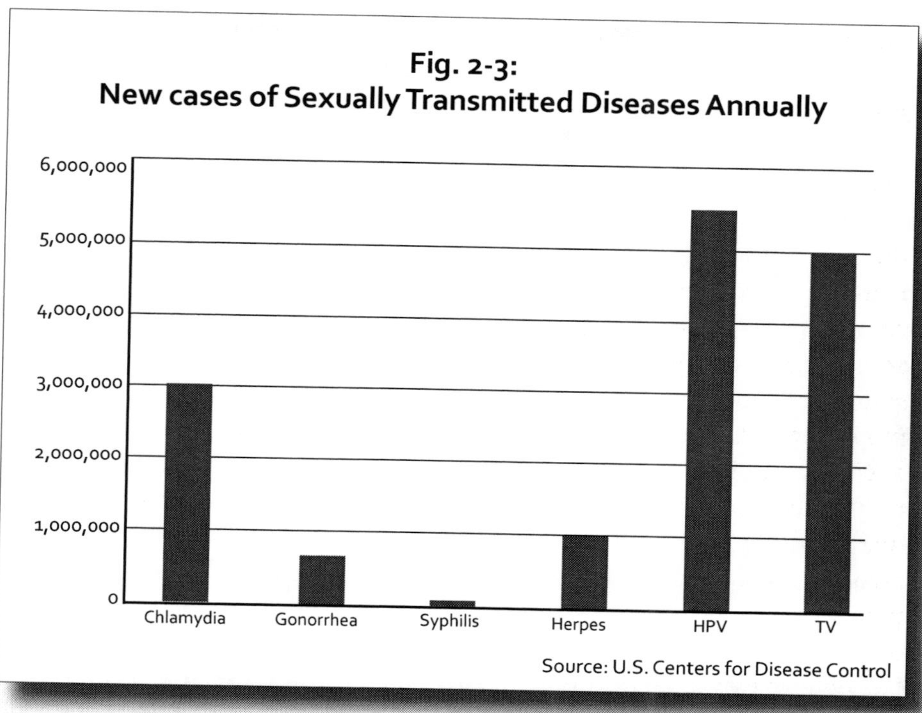

See Chapter Four for detailed information on these and other Sexually Transmitted Diseases.

their children from harmful influences they might stumble upon while surfing the web.

• Open a dialogue with your teenagers about how society objectifies people. Unfortunately, it's not too difficult to find examples of this in our society. Ask them to try to "empathize" with someone who's been used for monetary gain. (Money drives the pornography industry.)

• Explain the difference between "lust" and "love." Explain the importance of remaining chaste. Teach chastity as a virtue.

• Brainstorm ideas for dating that allow teenagers to channel their passions in positive ways.

• Encourage your son to define a "rite of passage" that doesn't have a sexual component. Perhaps it can be a physical accomplishment like climbing a mountain or running in a marathon.

• Again, encourage girls not to dress so they inspire lurid thoughts in young men.

Hooking up

A devastating trend creeping around us is the idea of casual, no-strings-attached sexual encounters. It's called "hooking up" and if you haven't heard of it yet, you will!

Years ago, a "hook up" was the expression my friends and I used when we wanted to meet, as in "let's hook up at the bowling alley after dinner." Today, "hooking up" describes a couple of friends getting together for casual sex. No strings; no consequences. Can there be such an act?

Sex carries consequences and has moral implications – always! Whether or not we're willing to admit it, our attitudes about sex reveal our moral integrity. Sexual relations must be contained within the gift of marriage to be considered moral. Casual sex is illegitimate. It's a lie.

If you buy into the idea that a "hook up" between friends is okay, you are being bamboozled by a society that worships commerce. Yes commerce. In her book, *Smart Sex*, Jennifer Roback Morse writes that if you view your sex partner exclusively as a source for pleasure, "you are reducing him or her to a consumer good." Thus, the world of commerce enters the bedroom.

I believe this need to "hook up" stems from a more serious problem affecting our country — fear. Americans are deeply afraid. This fear isn't the result of recent world events; it didn't originate with the terrorists attacks on September 11, 2001. Rather, what Americans fear most – dependence – is an affliction that's been centuries in the making. Since the time of the American Revolution, this country has held up independence as its fundamental ideal. The strong choose independence while the weak settle for dependence. Pointing to this ideology has led some people to proclaim that dependence upon God is proof of a person's weakness. Even a former governor of Minnesota, Jessie Ventura, went on record with his opinion that "religion is a crutch."

When people fear dependence, they also fear the perception of dependence. Where does this fear lead? It leads to people who are afraid to commit to a single, life-long relationship. It leads to a child who is afraid to remain dependent upon parents even though parents hold the child's best interest in their hearts. It also leads to parents who don't want to become dependent upon adult children. (Not wanting to "be a burden" on children is a common sentiment among the elderly). By avoiding "dependence" people can achieve the American ideal of independence while totally missing God's purpose for humanity.

God wants us to be dependent on Him – and on each other. The ability to create a lasting relationship with another person is a human attribute, a human strength. So why are people afraid to do just that? Is it because too many among us have decided to turn away from the authority of God and seek our own counsel, something we're woefully ill-equipped to do?

The most vocal among us will point their fingers to the cross and cry foul. They'll say humans don't need "symbols" to find strength. They'll say strength can be found within. But we need God. *We need God.*

"A society that defines freedom as the absence of unconditionally committed human relationships cannot remain free. And individuals who define freedom in this way are abandoning the very thing that has the best chance of making them happy," Roback Morse writes. So as people tout free sex as a societal good, really they are becoming a slave and dooming themselves to an unhappy life.

Sexual relationships, which connect one person to another, are not casual but committed sex, which is cherished by married couples all over the world. Sex carries the potential of making adults uniquely and totally aware of another person. It feeds concern for the other's well being. Sex involves people and people have feelings, whether we like it or are willing to admit it – or not. There is no denying that sex affects human emotion.

Roback Morse writes that a free society requires people with a conscience. When you think back through history, and you need to go no farther back than the twentieth century, the most notorious leaders who fought against freedom were the same leaders who clearly led without conscience — Hitler, Stalin, and Mussolini are examples.

As we teach our children about the world, we need to teach more than feelings. We need to talk about things like conscience and values and we need to help them make clear distinctions – right and wrong assessments – about thoughts and acts in order to help our children choose the "true freedom" of a life lived within Christ. Children need to learn that things that "feel" right may be deceiving. They also need to be taught that their own authority often cannot be trusted. Furthermore, moral indifference is equal to immorality.

You can no more accept the idea of casual sex or "hooking up" as you could encourage a daughter to pursue a life of prostitution or advocate polygamy for your son. Even Biblical texts that include polygamous relationships are wrought with stories of strained relations, disputes and jealousy.

And didn't Christ command the prostitute to "sin no more?"

In addition to the emotional outgrowth of a sexual relationship, our bodies release hormones that connect us to our partner physiologically and psychologically. These biologic responses to intercourse, which are explained in later chapters, underscore that sex is a gift God designed to

---

Linda and Dave's "Top Ten" Ways to Raise Godly Children

Raising godly children has always been a challenge, and until we come face-to-face with our Maker, it likely always will be. Is there a tried and true process by which parents can be guaranteed their children will become godly adults? While I wish I could say there was – and that my husband, Dave, and I have mastered it – it just isn't possible. Each person is unique and endowed with a free will, therefore, we can only help each other and keep trying our best.

For fun, I have developed a "top ten" list of things our family has done in an effort to instill godly values in our children. We don't claim that we have the secret to raising godly children or that we are perfect parents, but we do take parenting seriously. And, we have a sense of humor. I hope you find a tip or two among the list that can help your family.

1. Breastfeed them. Breastfeeding is the best way to begin the parental nurturing process. This nurturing does not evaporate once babies are weaned. Children who were breastfed as babies will remain close to parents because of the early bond that developed during breastfeeding. Furthermore, children who witness siblings being breastfed will observe a terrific model of sacrificial giving. Breastfeeding helped teach our children what love is and who loves them.

2. Feed them well and eat with them. While this may seem rather obvious, it isn't to some families. There are many families who do not cook daily, nutritious family meals or sit down to eat with each other! A study has just been published, which shows teenage girls are less likely to experience eating disorders when they eat at least five meals a week with their family.[14] I understand that families today are busier than ever. No matter! Rearrange mealtime if you must so that you and your children can share at least one nutritious home-cooked meal per day.

3. Clothe them. I have a problem with giving children an allowance. At our house, we provide our children what they need rather than allowing them to save an allowance to buy things of their choosing. Parents surrender their power to veto purchases once they've handed money over to their children. What often happens is purchases become the source of conflict between children and parents. Part of the parenting challenge in teaching children to be consumers, of course, is teaching

accompany the covenant of marriage.

Your marriage covenant has brought forth children who may choose, as you have, to follow God and His plan for us. Or, your children may turn their backs on Him. Their decision to love, trust and keep true to the faith will be communicated through their choices. Like it or not, those choices

---

the difference between a need and a want.

4. **Pray for them**. It seems obvious, but it isn't for some. Furthermore, teach them to pray for you so you are strengthened in your endeavors. Parenting is hard work and you need Godly inspiration and support. Growing up in today's world is challenging so prayer is a must.

5. **Model godliness.** Teens and young children model what they see. If you find yourself complaining about your children, perhaps what's needed is a deep look within for signs of personal ungodliness. Rooting out our own bad habits can go a long way toward molding "godliness" in our children. Godliness hosts a peace that is apparent to the observer; children will be drawn to us when we model godliness and peace that comes from trying to act as God acts.

6. **Help them**. Help your children even when they don't ask for help. This doesn't mean doing things for them that would serve to make them grow and mature. Helping or assisting children unexpectedly may make their day. It can also help you connect in unanticipated ways. We all love it when someone else helps us unexpectedly or acts generously. Make yourselves available for your children in the same way and the payback will be enormous. It is in giving that we receive... .

7. **Nurture them**. Ponder this comment: "Hurt people hurt people. Loved people love people."

8. **Work them.** Like adults, children and teenagers need to feel productive and to be creatively engaged with challenging projects. They also shouldn't always be on the receiving end in your household. When you are busy with household chores, they should be too, in proportion to their age and ability. Keeping children busy has many benefits: they learn new tasks; you may complete a project faster, and the task just might be more fun when worked on together.

9. **Rein over your household.** Rein as a benevolent king and queen rules over their subjects — with love and concern for their well being. It is easier to understand rules, and abide by them, when you know you are loved.

10. **Love them unconditionally**. God asks that we follow in His footsteps. God loves us unconditionally; we are called to love as He does. While some days this can be challenging, it is our duty.

---

depend greatly on how effectively you help your children avoid the landmines that society has placed in their path.

The underlying sin that gives the landmines presented in this chapter their explosive quality is lust. The cardinal virtue that opposes the sin of lust is chastity. As you develop a battle plan to protect your children from the lures of immodest dress or the temptation of pornography and sex outside of marriage, know that you are building a coat of arms for them that will protect their chastity and bring them closer to Christ. Under the scope of eternity, a chastity lesson aimed at a teen will prove far more valuable to a child's life than a lesson in American history that includes nationalistic ideals such as freedom, independence and the pursuit of happiness.

God wants us all to live our lives according to His plan. He has given us His teachings, the Church and grace to help us succeed in His plan for us. Additionally, He's given the world the wonderful gift of teenagers, in all their boundless enthusiasm. Muster the fortitude to harness their energy and send it in the right direction. Toward Christ. ❦

chapter three

Speaking on Gender

Is it so great to be a woman in this day and age? Is it great to be a man, for that matter? Have you ever wondered which gender is better? The last question sounds rather ridiculous if you believe like me that all people – men and women – are God's creatures and created as equals in His sight.

Psalm 139 describes our creation beautifully: "*You formed my inmost being / you knit me in my mother's womb / I praise you, so wonderfully you made me / wonderful are your works! / My very self you knew; / my bones were not hidden from you, / when I was being made in secret, / fashioned as in the depths of the earth. / Your eyes foresaw my actions; / in your book all are written down, / my days were shaped before one came to be. / How precious to me are your designs, O God; / how vast the sum of them!*"

When you ask yourself what it means to be a woman or a man you might be compelled to ponder God's purpose for your existence. During prayer, you may ask Him: "Why was I created?" or more specifically, "Why was I created as a woman (or man) loaded with talents and gifts, which were freely given, not earned. Then welcome your femininity or masculinity as a true gift.

God is neither male nor female; He is spirit with a perfect mind and will. God is three divine persons in one: Father, Son and Holy Spirit.

How then, your child might ask, can we say people are made in His image and likeness when people have bodies but God doesn't? The response can be as simple as this explanation offered by Father Richard Hogan: "We are made in the image of likeness of God precisely because we are persons with a mind and a will – as is He. Further, our bodies are to express our persons, the powers of our mind and will. Thus, our bodies are the outward, visible expression of our persons, our minds and wills."

A human uses the intellect to reason through a situation; he or she then communicates the results of that thought process through an action taken by the body. Thus, our bodies are fundamental to God's plan of creation because it is through our bodies – through our actions – that we reveal His mastery and glory. Sadly, it is also through our bodies that we tell God we reject His plan for us.

Catholic priests John LeVoir and Richard Hogan in their book, *Faith for Today*, write about how our human bodies are inextricably linked to our souls: "We received our bodies as part and parcel of the gift of life ... they are created to be the expressions of our persons. In other words, there is a fundamental unity in each of our persons. We are body and soul, but the two are united as one. In this duality, we confront one of the essential mysteries about man. It should not surprise us that man is a mystery." Man, as enigma, also reflects his creator.

But what should we make of gender differences? If God is at work in creation, why did He bother making men *and* women? God could have kept creating one person at a time as he had Adam and Eve; certainly He didn't need to give people the ability to co-create more people. Yet God *has* given us the ability to create *with* him. This implies that I, a woman, and my husband Dave, a man, have been engendered for a very specific purpose — to unite and bring forth children in partnership with God.

At the moment of creation – at conception – the physical "mortal" flesh is enjoined to the spiritual "immortal" soul to create a new human person. Through God's design, man and woman merge biologically at conception to create the "mortal" being while God is present to breathe His existence, or the "immortal" being, into new life. This is God's design for human creation and it cannot be altered or improved upon through technology or "enlightened" thinking. It is perfect.

In situations where conception occurs under less than perfect or even dire circumstances, such as the case following rape, life still emerges as a result of His design. Thus all life, regardless of the circumstance surrounding its conception, receives the gift of a soul because of His unconditional love. All life, therefore, should be viewed as God-given — deserving of both protection and respect.

In recent years, scientific developments have given people the opportunity to pursue conception outside of the human person. This technology creates moral paradox because, in essence, it appears to give people god-like power over life and death – control they were never designed to wield or assume. The most obvious question which results from science-enabled conception is this: When a scientist "creates" a person in a Petri dish, how will he or she or others hang onto the conviction that the wee person they illicitly made nevertheless embodies a soul from God? The irony here is that even in this instance, God *is* the Creator who breathes immortal souls into all new life, (an ordered process of His creation) even a life who is helped into being at the hands of a scientist working in a laboratory. This immortality, while outside a person's control, is embedded into our very being. But deeper, more troubling issues also arise from the process of artificial reproduction.

In Pope John Paul II's *Theology of the Body*, he writes: "The various techniques of artificial reproduction which would seem to be at the service of life and which are frequently used with this intention, actually open the door to new threats against life. Apart from the fact that they are morally unacceptable, since they separate procreation from the fully human context of the conjugal act, these techniques have a high rate of failure: not just failure in relation to fertilization but with regard to the subsequent development of the embryo which is exposed to the risk of death, generally within a very short space of time. Furthermore, the number of embryos produced is often greater than that needed for implantation in the woman's womb, and these so-called 'spare embryos' are then destroyed or used for research which, under the pretext of scientific or medical progress, in fact reduces human life to the level of simple 'biological material' to be freely disposed of."

I met a woman several years ago who shared with me her struggle with infertility and how she and her husband resolved it through artificial reproduction. For this family, the laboratory-based fertilization process created about twenty embryos. Ten embryos were implanted first but only two survived resulting in the birth of twins; six embryos were implanted a few years later and the result was the birth of a single child. Four embryos, she told me that day, still floated in a cryogenic bath waiting for her to decide whether or not to implant again. The woman seemed genuinely troubled as she faced the decision over what to do with the "babies" she had waiting for her at the laboratory now that her first three babies had grown into active little boys. On that particular day, she no longer believed she wanted more children.

I recall wondering what would lead a person to the point where they could consider damning their offspring to frozen limbo, or worse, to certain death. (Some have suggested these "frozen" persons should be adoptable.) In this woman's case, the same technology that conveniently allowed her to achieve pregnancy quickly became inconvenient as she found herself having to ponder uncomfortable, unexpected choices that made her question fundamental beliefs about the value of bringing these embryos to "life."

I think she read the shock that came over my face as I listened to her quickly rationalize her feelings by saying, "these embryos probably wouldn't make it anyway." This woman's experience is a clear example of what Pope John Paul II meant when he said that while artificial reproduction appears to serve life it actually opens the door to death.

Other Orwellian dilemmas have risen from artificial reproduction technology. Today, couples pursuing in-vitro fertilization have the opportunity to select the gender of their offspring. This sex selection occurs during a laboratory process called "sperm washing" where male fertilized eggs are separated from female fertilized eggs before implantation into a woman's uterus. For couples desiring a child of a certain gender, what becomes of the embryos not qualifying?

It used to be, couples facing a diagnosis of infertility had two options: they could adopt, or they could adapt to a childless life together. Today, science allows infertile couples to believe only time and money stand between them and "achieving pregnancy." While the monetary costs to pursue artificial reproduction are high, the emotional, physical, psychological and moral costs are staggering. There are societal costs as well, paid by hundreds of thousands of future humans who are "disposed of" in the interest of science and the millions of people who accept this, label it progress.

Christ, through His Church, calls all married couples to be open to life in their marital commitment. Although this call necessarily rejects all behaviors and contraception methods that close the door to life, it doesn't mean couples can't learn about their bodies and use that knowledge to space their children according to their family's needs. (See Chapter Eight for information on natural family planning.) The Church helps us understand why we must reject any illicit artificial means to achieve pregnancy. (The Church continues to study the many scientific ways to help couples that are experiencing fertility issues achieve pregnancy. The Church teaches that conception must take place in the privacy of the mother's body for the protection of all involved. Also a baby deserves to be co-created with the genetic material of it's mother and father. It can be said generally that processes that *assist* natural conception (within the mother's body) are licit whereas processes that replace a natural conception are illicit and disrespect the dignity of the emerging new life as well as that of husband and wife. According to God's plan, new life is God's gift to a husband and wife and their gift to each other and God. When we love God and each other authentically, we remain open to this gift.

On that same note, we have done nothing to warrant our sexual gender or the gender of our children; rather, maleness or femaleness is ordained by God. For all of the great advances in biology that have given society processes for artificial reproduction, embryo implantation, in-vitro fertilization, sex selection, even surrogate motherhood, science has not yet been able to construct or appreciate the essence of the whole person – the intellect, the soul (including free will) and the body. Human beings are incapable of replicating or reproducing the soul. Our souls exist beyond what can be touched or manipulated; they belong to God because they come from God.

In our increasingly secular world, gender has lost much of its significance. Our laws regard men and women equally and, if some have their way, marriage will be redefined to include male-male or female-female unions. Society does a fine job touting the benefits of "diversity" as it encourages us to embrace questionable ideals while at the same time it wants to blur any distinctions between men and women so we become, in essence, interchangeable. No longer are Americans encouraged to celebrate the differences between men and women as we did in 1973 during the famous "battle of the sexes" tennis match between Bobby Riggs and Billie Jean King. Gender, at least in the secular world, is a non-issue.

Of course, gender begs differences in the areas of pregnancy, childbirth and breastfeeding and has thus become a flashpoint for feminists who dismiss women's reproductive and nurturing roles because they can't balance those roles with their cries for equality.

In relation to our souls, gender also matters. While men and women are made equally in the image and likeness of God and both are made fully human by God, our gender matters because of His design for our lives and our bodies. The human body – both male and female – is the sum of its biological functions, plus a whole lot more. Yet, we obviously differ from one another. Scientists, while being able to study the biological aspects that form our gender, haven't been able to wrap their studies, analysis, or tests around the "more" part of our humanity — the mysterious nature of our intellect and will.

The female sex

One of the twentieth century's great thinkers, G.K. Chesterton, looked at the difference between men and women in a review of Louisa Alcott's masterpiece *Little Women*. Chesterton writes: "wisdom, first and last, is the characteristic of women. They are often silly, they are always wise. Commonsense is uncommon among men; but commonsense is really and literally a common sense among women. And the sagacity of women, like the sagacity of saints, or that of donkeys is something outside all questions of ordinary cleverness and ambition."

Chesterton's description of women as keenly perceptive is reinforced by Dr. Ellen Grant in her book *Sexual Chemistry.* She writes: "In general, women are more intuitive, sociable, talkative and interested in a wide range of issues." Clearly, women are sensitive beings; they discern information about the world through their senses.

Historically, women have assumed the role of nurturer within the family, nurturer defined as one who furthers the development of another. Of course, this is exactly what happens in the womb during pregnancy; a woman gives her fetus nourishment, time and protection to grow and develop until the point of birth. But infants don't stop needing their mothers once they emerge into daylight. For eighteen to twenty years after birth, children will look to their mothers for nourishment —physical, emotional and spiritual, — for protection and the time necessary to mature into adulthood. Because women are naturally intuitive, clever and ambitious, they are uniquely qualified to oversee the development of their offspring.

In the 1960s, women picked up the fight for equality demanding, among other things, equal pay for equal work. While on the surface of it, pay equity seems an achievement worthy of a battle, one result of achieving protections for workplace equity has been the devaluation of women's work in the home – specifically the work of raising children. It has been decades since the quest for equal opportunities for women in the workplace touched off heated debates and today society not only accepts that women add value to the marketplace, it encourages them to abandon non-salaried work — mothering, for instance — in order to pursue a more "rewarding" career, reward being defined in secular, often monetary terms.

But what's more rewarding: a paycheck handed over after forty hours spent missing your baby's first steps, or an afternoon spent cuddling and reading to your toddler, giving him the nourishment and security he needs to develop into a strong, confident young man? Women everywhere are being deluded when they are told that raising their children is less important than contributing to the marketplace.

Here's Chesterton again, writing in *Brave New Family:* "It may be emancipation to allow a woman to make part of a pin, if she really wants to make part of a pin. But we question whether it is really a more human achievement to make part of a pin than to make the whole of a pinafore. And we even go further, and question whether it is more human to make the whole of a pinafore than to look after the whole of a child."

Pinafores have fallen out of fashion and, sadly, so too has the burning desire in most women to stay home to raise their children. In a society that promotes sameness (yet calls it diversity), women are told they can be interchangeable with men *but only in the marketplace*, and it has guaranteed equity under law, *but only in the marketplace*! Women who reject this call to pursue equity with men, choosing instead to place their children and households ahead of "career achievement" are subsequently devalued. How ironic! The whole of these women's contribution to society can't be measured by economists because it's truly invaluable. Yet women at home very rarely get credit for the work they do – and it is difficult, oftentimes thankless work.

Women are nurturers by nature, and nature is God's intention revealed. How sad for our children, and society as a whole, that women who work outside the home are often pitted against their sisters who work inside the home, each trying to prove their contributions have value. God loves all women, in all their weaknesses and faults. The debate whether it's better for women to work outside the home or stay home and raise children will rage on beyond the pages of this book. But I encourage all women to stop fighting one another over their choices and act in faith and love as God intended. Women should no more deny their nature than they should deny that the female gender should never be promoted as "equal" to the male gender. Women and men are not the same; they're just loved equally by God.

The male sex

Throughout history, men have widely been regarded as the "head of the household" – a label which has grown quite negative in its connotation in recent years as people assume it implies men wield power over the household, and thus, over women. Again, I turn to Chesterton, who explains that men were referred to as "head of a house" because it is the head that does the talking. "The father of the family has never been called 'king of the house' or 'priest of the house,' or 'pope of the house,'" Chesterton asserts. "His power was not dogmatic or definite enough for that." Where men are considered "head," Chesterton wrote, women complement men by acting as "heart of the house." Chesterton's description of men's and women's roles within the "body of the house" teems with life. With man as the head and woman as the heart, it's easy to see God's handiwork within the family.

But how else do men differ from women? For one thing, the anatomies of men's brains differ from women's. And their brains function differently partly due to the release of different hormones. Dr. Grant explains that while women are intuitive, men tend to be interested in technicalities. Men like machines and excel in math; they pursue knowledge of how things work. "Men are more able to keep judgments and emotion separate and are less able to voice their emotions. Men have better abstract mathematical and spatial abilities and are more likely to be composers and technicians," writes Grant. The reason, Grant asserts, is anatomical; it's because the right half of men's brains are well developed.

Women, on the other hand, derive their intuition from better connections between their right brain and their left brain.

Other physical differences between the sexes can be traced to testosterone, an anabolic (increases constructive metabolism) hormone. Because men produce testosterone, they are more muscular and have larger bones and brains than women of comparable age. A larger brain doesn't equal higher intelligence, however. Each part of the brain functions differently with the release of hormones playing a key role.

Testosterone also plays a role in the fetal development of males. As early as five to six weeks after conception, a normally-developing male will receive a surge of testosterone, which is taken in by sensitive testosterone receptors in the brain, which triggers genital development. This normal development can be thwarted if key nutrients, such as zinc, are in short supply or if female hormones are ingested by the mother. Genetically male infants who have not received adequate testosterone at key moments during brain development will not develop normal male genitalia.

The differences between the sexes can be traced to testosterone, an anabolic hormone. Because men produce testosterone, they are more muscular and have larger brains and bones than women.

Under the influence of specific sex hormones – testosterone for men and estrogen for women – the gender of a fetus is determined. If, during early pregnancy, a woman ingests estrogen, her genetically male baby can be born with female-type genitalia. Problems with developing male genitalia also can occur if the mother ingests testosterone or progesterone. I know of a case in which a woman, unknowingly pregnant, ingested birth control pills for the full term of her pregnancy. Her son was born with a severely underdeveloped penis and testicles; the boy must take testosterone shots indefinitely.

Ultimately, the difference between male and female can be considered great, or minute. You may think of men as large, strong, vocal and protective; you may regard women as petite, intuitive, kind and nurturing. Or, you may view the differences between the sexes as slight – a carbon atom here, a hydrogen atom there and, voila – a man can become a woman. Sometimes, the study of anatomy reduces humans to the sum of their respective parts and as I stated earlier, scientists have been very adept at explaining humans until they get to the "more" part. Women are nurturing and a whole lot more! Men are strong and a whole lot more!

Men and women, by their human nature, were created in the image and likeness of God. And they are called to be in relationship with God. No matter how hard society pushes women to achieve equality, i.e., maleness, no matter how hard women push men to find their feminine side, i.e., sensitivity, there's no accepting the notion that men and women — individual reflections of their Creator – are interchangeable.

It is God's plan for men to complement women and women to complete men. Men and women are engendered differently in order to fulfill God's plan to bring forth new life through the act in which they unconditionally give of themselves – the marital embrace. Through Grace received at the Sacrament of Marriage, a man and woman give themselves to one another in order to express their life-giving love to each other and to God. As we contemplate the "why" of our gender, we're led back to the will of the Creator. Accepting that you're made in the image and likeness of God should lead you to conclude that His gift of gender for your design is part of His plan for you! When a married man and woman express their love for one another and their embrace is complete and open to life, this unconditional love for each other is returned to them. Furthermore, their unconditional love becomes a gift to God, and God blesses us for our gifts to Him. This is what it means to express our gender in a very personal, God-like way.

Homosexuality: Gender disordered

The influence of hormones on sexual development is clear. Sometimes, though, hormone imbalances occur during the critical stages of brain development which may result in sexual disorientation. This disorientation may be manifested as homosexual identity. Psychologists and others have not been able to identify the exact reasons why some individuals are homosexual; some claim environmental causes whereas others list genetic or behavioral reasons.

It is not a sin to be a homosexual; sin occurs through actions such as when one performs an act of homosexuality. Fr. Richard Hogan in a booklet he prepared for NFP teachers in 1999 titled *John Paul II's New Vision of Human Sexuality, Marriage and Family Life,* explains: "In marriage, two people, a man and a woman, give themselves to each other and this self-donation is expressed in and through their bodies. They become one flesh.

This is possible because of the differences in masculinity and femininity. However, it is impossible for two people of the same gender to become one flesh...Homosexuals' acts are sins against love because homosexual acts purport to be expressions of a bodily union which cannot exist. Further, there is no possibility for new life. Homosexual acts therefore are not acts of love. Two of the characteristics of love are missing: the total self-gift of one person to the other expressed in and through a bodily union; and the possibility of new life."

Men and women, regardless of gender or "gender orientation" are faced with the same quandary: choose to live according to His will (following His commandments), or, reject His word and live life according to whim. This is the essence of this thing called free will.

Homosexuals may argue that those who oppose their "sexual identity" or "choice of life partner" deny them fundamental rights to love and marry as they choose. Often, the word "discrimination" is bandied about within the debate to sanctify gay marriage. Yet *sacramental* marriage is not a man-made institution; it's a covenant between a man, a woman, and God. God instituted marriage for a man and a woman to give themselves to each other permanently and completely; sexually cementing their union, while simultaneously contributing to creation. Within a marital sexual union, a man and a woman come together to become whole – therefore a reflection of God. No doubt you've heard the expression *the two become one?*

Two males (or two females) cannot complete a sexual union that was designed for one man and one woman. As Father Hogan said, in the absence of two genders coming together as one, an act purported as an act of love is merely an act of lust — harmful and destructive. Men and women were designed to complement one another, to become one body with man as the head and woman as the heart. Without understanding the complementary nature of male joined to female, homosexuals confuse love with pleasure; they fail to understand (or accept) God's design for love and marriage. They will never exclaim with joy in the way that Adam did in Genesis 3:23: *"This one, at last, is bone of my bones and flesh of my flesh; / this one shall be called 'woman,' for out of 'her man' this one has been taken."* The passage goes on: *"it's for this reason a man leaves his father and mother and clings to his wife, and the two of them become "one body."*

Some homosexuals have argued that because God had His hand in their design (which is true) they must be "true" to their design and their identity by acting out their homosexuality. But this is false logic. Homosexual activity is disordered from the Creator's plan regardless of the root cause, whether it be biologic or some type of environmental **or** familial dysfunction. A person who pairs with one of the same gender for sexual activity denies the truth and meaning behind God's design for men and women.

For younger children, the image of a jig saw puzzle whose pieces are not cut to fit together (to reflect physical and spiritual love) is a useful way to explain the disorder of homosexuality. When discussing homosexuality with older teens, remind them that sometimes our own biological design acts like a detour that blocks the road to fulfilling God's will. But prayer and grace, received through the Sacraments, can help people with homosexual leanings stay on track.

Contraception, another late twentieth century development that purports to improve the male-female relationship, actually serves to disrupt gender roles. Since the introduction of birth control pills, studies reveal gender has become muddled because one sex has gained control over the reproductive process and children have effectively been eliminated from God's order of creation. (See Chapter Nine for a complete discussion on contraception).

Our youngest daughter, Kyra, has Down Syndrome. Her condition is the result of a biological disorder – not the plan of the Father and yet within the plan of the Father! Yet I must teach Kyra the fullness of the faith with the expectation that she, just like her brothers and sisters, must live her life in accord with God's law – not her own. The challenges that spring from her disorder do not exempt her from God's plan. I expect from Kyra the same obedience to God's will that I expect from my other children.

The truth is, homosexual acts are sinful in the same fashion as heterosexual acts conducted outside of marriage or marital acts that thwart authentic love by being purposely closed to life. God's law for homosexuals is the same as it is for all unmarried people – prayer, faith in God, and abstinence.

Many tend to regard gender differences as a conflict: man versus woman rather than complementary as man *and* woman. We need to get back to the understanding that men and women are designed to complement each other. How much better would it be for our world if men and women traveled down the path of life together instead of one out front, the other lagging behind, the two engaged in perpetual competition? Gender wars serve only to exacerbate the problems in our society. Society would be better served if men and women worked in concert to seek solutions to the problems of their families.

In my own family, I often marvel at how my husband, Dave, and I arrive at a solution to a problem neither of us could have solved individually. This is just one byproduct of a complementary relationship. I'm doubtful we could handle significant challenges within our family if either of us approached the other with arrogance or pride, arguing that one of us is better, smarter, more creative, more intuitive, etc.; these are the claims that fuel arguments between spouses. When couples attack a problem together by interjecting ideas that pour from the wellspring of their gender, however, I'm confident their solutions will likely bring them close to where God intended them to be.

The further "enlightened" our society becomes, as more and more people decide to follow their "own" design instead of God's, the easier it becomes to ignore the spiritual and theological dimension of the human person and rationalize certain behaviors.

Men and women are given free will to choose actions that fulfill our Creator's intentions; we can reflect His will by emphasizing the wonderful complementary design of human gender. When Chesterton states that man is the head of the house and woman is the heart, I conclude that it is children who compose the remainder of the body of Christ to round us into complete people. When children are removed from – or even estranged from – our description of the family, it becomes harder for the head and heart to get along.

Male-female relationships certainly have changed in my lifetime and it's harder and harder to teach children that gender matters and there are differences between men and women. It is the complementary nature of man and woman that makes us happy. The truth is, God made men and He made women and His purpose is clear: a man leaves his father and mother and clings to his wife, and the two of them become one. ❦

chapter four

Patient: Heal Thyself

Several years ago, a student attending one of our natural family planning classes had a change of heart concerning her chosen method of birth control. She'd been using an intrauterine device (IUD) but after attending our class decided to stop using this contraceptive device to space her babies. Instead, she adopted natural family planning. In essence, her heart opened to God's plan for her life and as a result, she no longer could tolerate the presence of an IUD in her body.

When the woman visited her doctor and asked him to remove the IUD, he urged her to reconsider. Christmas was approaching, he reminded her, with all its celebrations and holiday festivities. To remove her IUD at this time would surely result in an unintended pregnancy followed by a flood of regret. He also suggested to her that her change in attitude was the result of her not thoroughly understanding the consequences of choosing to abandon her IUD.

Yet she did, in fact, perfectly understand the consequences of her decision. Through our class, she learned that IUDs prompt the lining of a woman's uterus, the endometrium, to release leukocytes and prostaglandins making it inhospitable to sperm and/or a newly conceived life. The presence of a foreign object (such as an IUD) inside the uterus can prevent embryo implantation; the result: an early stage abortion. Acting in this dual fashion means intrauterine devices have both a contraceptive and an abortifacient potential. Consequently, IUDs can be used for "emergency contraception" within five days of having unprotected sexual intercourse, when primary contraception was forgotten or had failed, i.e., a condom broke. The IUD is touted to be more than 99 percent effective when used in these situations – a higher degree of effectiveness than emergency contraception pills. As a result of that knowledge, our student realized that her use of the IUD may have resulted in the death of her babies.

First generation IUDs have been largely removed from the market but a flood of second generation IUDs and abortifacients in the form of pills, shots, implants, and patches have been developed and gained acceptance in the marketplace. (See Chapter nine for more on fertility.)

How sad for this woman, and countless others, that her doctor focused only on the physical consequences of her decision and failed to recognize that his patient's focus had shifted; the moral and spiritual consequences of her actions were now included in her primary concerns. Her story illustrates how inept the medical community can be when attempting to address "whole person" issues, decisions that affect the physical, the spiritual — and most importantly — the eternal.

Can we set the blame for this doctor's attitude solely at his feet, or those within the medical community? Probably not. While there are many physicians who support women who've rejected chemical birth control, these doctors clearly fall into the minority. Most physicians treat patients without concern for moral issues – they practice medicine under the auspices of civil statutes and corporate health organization mandates that demand they treat patients in an environment free from religious influence. Under such a system, a physician who encounters a person engaged in risky behaviors can focus only on consequence mitigation. They may offer protections from disease or detours around probable results, but they ignore the full picture: the spiritual, physical and psychological consequences and root causes of risky behavior. Instead, they stand silent when they easily could take a moral stand that might serve as a life-altering moment for their patient. Instead, they fall short of making value judgments that might be construed as offensive. Our society frowns on those who might take a moral stand on another's actions – even physicians.

Yet every person's actions will eventually impact society, regardless of the ubiquitous philosophy of "live and let live." As a society, we must be willing to uphold common moral principles. If not, we are sure to suffer.

As a parent, I am sometimes told I am too strict with my children. This assessment doesn't surprise me considering how parents today often have their authority usurped by those who espouse the "it takes a village" approach to parenting. (People who feel they do better with your children than you.) Am I a perfect parent? Hardly. Are my children perfect? No, they sometimes make bad choices or do inappropriate things. Yet if I do my job correctly and impose consequences on their actions, they will learn quickly from their errors. I never want to hear that I didn't do enough, didn't care enough, didn't take the time necessary to teach and use discipline when it was called for! Parents must not pretend that their children's bad behavior wasn't *that* bad or give excuses for misbehavior – especially when some consequences are inevitable, purely by nature of our human design.

Adolescence is an opportune developmental stage whereby parents can positively influence and affect behaviors and attitudes, further impact their children's developing moral character, and hopefully circumvent problem behaviors. Furthermore, adolescence is an opportunity for parents to redirect their children toward constructive activities.

Adolescence is an opportune developmental stage whereby parents can positively influence children's attitudes and behavior.

It's not that peers *pull* away from their parents during the teen years; rather, it can be parents themselves who *push* adolescents toward their peers by failing to monitor their children, by being too busy or disengaged to provide supervision, and by failing to hold children accountable. Of course, parents themselves may feel insecure or helpless; or, parents are in denial, pretending not to see what's obvious. Some parents have personal, psychological or physical problems that prevent them from being the role model they need to be for their children.

While parents come in all shapes and sizes, psychologists tell us that effective parents exhibit many similarities: they monitor their children diligently; they are consistent in setting rules and enforcing meaningful consequences; and they are neither authoritarian nor wishy-washy. Furthermore, parents need to be in agreement with one another about negative and positive behaviors, which ones they'll tolerate and which ones they won't. Successful parents also shower their children with praise, emotional support and love. They stay connected by communicating a desire to maintain a loving relationship.

Some adolescents and teens nevertheless rebel against their loving parents. What do they do then? Ron Fagan writes in *Counseling and Treating Adolescents:* "Some adolescents are willing to go to the very extreme to win a battle for control against their parents. Parents struggling for control must seek help from external sources, such as Christian counseling, school officials, treatment facilities, even the police."

Not long ago, a mother I know took her teenage daughter to Mexico for a vacation. The daughter didn't obey her curfew and instead went drinking with some local boys. Rather than clamping down on the daughter's behavior, the mother justified her inaction this way: "I couldn't ground her because she would've ruined my vacation. Besides she was just having fun!"

I doubt this mother would have looked the other way if she'd been fully informed about teen pregnancy rates, sexually transmitted infection rates, etc. All these dire consequences may result from teens *simply having fun*. This scenario repeats itself often when parents stop providing authority, good counsel, connectedness and love. All the evidence points to parental involvement, family support systems, family connections and religious influence as some of the most influential, positive factors affecting adolescent behavior! Yet some parent's today are very willing to hand over their parental authority to schools, legislators and physicians. They buy into the false mantras that dismiss the importance of parental influence to claim teenagers must have access to contraceptives (in their schools no less) otherwise they'll certainly face unintended pregnancies. Or, that abortion needs to be available on demand for teens (no parental controls allowed) because teenagers can't be relied upon to use contraceptives effectively.

It's the same convoluted thinking that leads us to prescribe diet pills for people who won't exercise, sleeping pills for people too stressed to get a good night's sleep, or provide clean needles to heroin addicts to reduce their chances of contracting AIDS. In all of these instances, the person's intellect – their free will to choose good over evil – is discounted; pleasure trumps truth. As another example of how schizophrenic this country approaches spirituality, look at how we treat criminals. Social justice advocates promote rehabilitation programs for criminals that almost always include a spiritual dimension and so there are chaplains in every prison. Yet, how many chaplains are available in public schools to impact children's formative years? Do public high schools allow teenagers to grow in their spiritual formation? None that I am aware of. Are they promoting abstinence education? Or, has it become easier to promote contraception from a school-based clinic than teach a child the discipline of self control?

These are challenges we all face – parents, teachers, counselors, priests, doctors, society as a whole. It's up to parents to retake the lead in their children's lives by promoting universal Judeo Christian standards and principled, dogmatic, objective values. Parents can't sit idle while schools, counselors, physicians and politicians espouse secularist and humanist philosophies with phony values. We shouldn't discard the ideal of living principled lives or leave God outside our inner circle.

We live in a culture of death and its influence upon us is dramatic. You are challenged to raise children while navigating this culture of death; the path is a treacherous one and society's mores can easily cloud your ability to see into the light of God's plan – His culture of life. Tread carefully!

Risky behaviors

Here we are in the twenty-first century still expecting our society to be happier than it is but settling for a world where STDs, teen pregnancies, poverty, crime, and immorality run rampant. I see societal problems as a consequence of men's and women's virtues and strengths being turned upside down or inside out. What used to be labeled a vice or bloodlust is now just another day in the neighborhood. Anything goes.

When diseases surface as a result of immoral activity, the medical community frequently adopts a risk "reduction" approach to treatment. Of course, a risk "elimination" approach would require a change in behavior. Yet people caught up in the culture of death often believe behavior modification is impossible. What's worse, many people conclude it doesn't matter. This is not true. People can change their actions and strengthen their character; it takes hard work, support and positive reinforcement from caring individuals – along with the intervention of grace and the Holy Spirit — to put down the doom-and-gloom and fear that weakens our resolve.

The statistics offered below are meant as a wake-up call for parents and teens. If your young person takes this information to heart because they are committed to living a godly life, then they will be better off for all of the right reasons. Others might find the information below enough to "scare" them into chastity. If that is the case, take heart. At least their fear will allow them more time to evaluate, observe and learn about the consequences and outcomes of different actions. Hopefully many will see that risky choices just aren't worth it. It is my further hope that all teenagers will choose to live in the culture of life and invite God into their tight circle of friends – with Him being at the top.

Building on ethics

There is a critical distinction between being an ethical person and one who has begun to embrace an understanding of actions and consequences based on *ethos*. Ethical children will obey in order to observe the law — not out of love but out of obligation. If a parent states a rule, an ethical child will follow the letter of the law usually by fixating on the exact phrasing as they heard it – sometimes without regard to trying to fully understand the intention behind the rule. On the other hand, children of *ethos* wish to understand why obedience is demanded of them; they want to understand what it is that their parents hope for them and to better understand why rules exist. *Ethos* (inner core development) allows children to see the importance of obedience in connection with love.

As you teach children obedience to you and God, show them how their actions have consequences above and beyond possible punishment for wrongdoing. Explain how their actions hurt themselves, and others, including God.

"Whatever you do to the least of these you do also to me."

Ethics has shallower roots than *ethos.* Decisions to abstain from risky behaviors should stem from a conviction to grow in holy, authentic love; love that never uses another; love that never allows ourselves to be used by others; and to grow in our understanding of God's Plan for us. A person of *ethos* is able to practice abstinence because of grace received from a loving God; choosing abstinence can be a teenager's gift back to God.

Risk reduction plays to ethics, not to *ethos*. Risk reduction techniques do not address the virtue of chastity. Rather, it focuses on the drugs or devices or techniques that reduce the likelihood of an unintended pregnancy or contraction of a sexually transmitted disease. And, reduce the likelihood of consequence is all risk reduction can do, for there is no single drug or device that will absolutely prevent a sexually active person from facing an unintended pregnancy or transmitting or contracting an STD. Abstinence is the only 100 percent effective way to avoid being trapped in the dangerous web cast by engaging in risky behavior.

Young people are gambling with their lives and hoping their luck holds. Yet, daily, many of these same teens lose those bets and the consequences can be significant. Consider the teen girl whose life is forever changed by an unintended pregnancy or the life-long health consequences of a STD picked up from a casual sexual encounter. Most girls don't understand how many health dangers they face beyond teenage pregnancy. They also fail to recognize that they are *more* at risk and bear greater consequences than their male counterparts. These increased risks and consequences simply can't be legislated or ruled away as some infer.

There are many health crises which befall young people who haven't heeded the call to chastity, self control and self discipline. They are outlined below. As parents, you want your children to grow into adulthood without having to face these challenges or have regrets. But you should also expect more from them. Don't just warn your children of the dangers of immoral behavior so they pass into adulthood filled with fear. Build your children's character so when they reach their teen years they choose abstinence and sexual purity and self control because they love you, they love themselves and they love God. Mold your children's character around embracing virtues rather than avoiding vices. This is partly how you'll instill in them *ethos* rather than simple ethics.

Tobacco, alcohol and other drugs

Tobacco is considered a gateway drug; this means it precedes and likely portends drug and alcohol use. Roughly 80 percent of teens who smoke for more than one year will be hooked for life, affecting their long term health. For Americans twelve years old and older in 2003, an estimated 71 million used tobacco products. This represents nearly one third of the U.S. population.

Alcohol and drug use by teens is a problem every community faces. Four out of five adolescents have consumed alcohol by the end of high school and nearly half of them, by the eighth grade. Two thirds of adolescents in twelfth grade and one-fifth of teenagers in eighth grade report having been drunk at least once in their life.[1]

Students wonder why they can't consume alcohol even though their parents do. Human brain development is partly the reason. "Adolescence represents a window of sensitivity. If the brain is exposed to certain chemicals during this period of development, it will be more detrimental to its health than if it were exposed to them at other times. The big danger for teens is addiction. Never will addiction to alcohol, drugs or smoking occur more quickly than during the teenage years. They are also much more resistant to recovery from these addictions."[2] Research shows that one binge drinking episode will negatively impair memory and learning for thirty days in teenagers. Furthermore, teen brains do not manifest signs of too much drinking as soon as adult brains; this compounds the problem and often results in over-drinking among teenagers.

Others tell us that: "Adolescence is a time of critical physical, mental and social, and psychological development compared to adulthood. Furthermore, the use of alcohol and drugs among adolescents is associated with the three highest causes of mortality among young people: physical injury (car accident, drowning), suicide, and homicide. Chronic use is often associated with other physiological, psychological and social problems, poor school and work performance, high risk health and sexual behavior, poor peer, family and community relations." [3]

Alcohol depresses the body's central nervous system and decreases brain activity. The consequence of this includes: increased depression, lowered inhibitions, and, impaired judgment. Impaired judgment and lowered inhibitions while under the influence of drugs and alcohol leads to early sexual initiation resulting in increased STDs and teen pregnancy. When used in combination with common over the counter (OTC) drugs such as acetaminophen, liver damage can occur, as well as the following problems: fainting, vomiting, nausea, and difficulty with breathing.

Furthermore, research suggests a connection between continued abuse of alcohol and drugs as adults. Ten percent to 35 percent carry drug and alcohol abuse into adulthood, the others abandon these risky behaviors after adolescence. This frequency may not sound alarming unless it involves your child or their friend(s); then any percent proves to be too high.

Illicit drugs

Drug abuse continues to be a major problem in the United States and it will remain a problem until accessibility pipelines are interrupted. Furthermore, substance abuse remains a temptation for adolescents who are depressed, have poor self-esteem, suffer from emotional or mental health issues, and who do not have healthy relationships with their parents.

Drug abuse can involve ingesting illegal (illicit) drugs; over-the-counter (OTC) or prescription (Rx) medications; or household chemicals used as inhalants such as aerosols, gasoline, paint and paint thinner. All are dangerous, with the latter group being particularly perilous because of its affordability and availability. Household inhalants often contain solvents and lead, which are poison and can cause brain damage and even death. A teen's perception of the risk of using inhalants is relatively low, according to the Partnership of a Drug Free America, which predicts "additional increase in use is expected." [4]

Marijuana is another *gateway* substance and it is the most widely used of all illicit drugs. WebMD reports 22 percent of teens currently use marijuana. Marijuana isn't as benign as some would like us to believe. It hinders memory, problem solving ability, learning, and causes mood swings, anxiety and depression. Pot is considered a gateway drug because users often move on to more dangerous, highly-addictive substances such as cocaine, methamphetamines, hallucinogens, and opiates.

Hallucinogens, opiates, meth, and cocaine have rightfully dangerous reputations; they are addictive and very dangerous to the user's mental and physical health. They have been known to cause seizures, psychosis, paranoia, hallucinations, strokes, etc. This reputation certainly reduces their use. WebMD cites 4 percent of teens use cocaine, 8 percent have used meth, 5 percent have used heroin and 7 percent have used Ecstasy, also known as the date rape drug. Ecstacy has been linked to liver damage and memory problems; it is particularly dangerous when combined with alcohol or other drugs.

In 2003, the American Academy of Child Adolescent Psychiatry estimated 19.5 million Americans aged twelve or older used illicit drugs. This represents 8.2 percent of the population. Furthermore, half of all teens, 51 percent, admitted to having tried an illicit drug by the time they finished high school and 17.3 percent of eighth graders report using a row inhalant at least once in their lifetime.[5] The good news is that a 2005 Partnership for a Drug-Free America survey confirms that "overall substance abuse is steadily declining among teens; use of tobacco, alcohol, marijuana, and ecstasy are all lower compared to earlier studies. But dangers lurk.

The Partnership for a Drug-Free America warns of a new kind of abuse: teens getting high from prescription medications such as Vicodin, OxyContin, Ritalin, and Adderall, and OTC medications like cough medications and others. These drugs are often accessible and affordable; they're found right in the medicine cabinets of many homes. It's easy to forget about old, left-over prescriptions sitting in the cabinet, but substance abuse experts warn us against letting down our guard. Nearly one in five teens, that's 20 percent, report abusing prescription medications and one in ten teens, 10 percent, report abusing cough medicine.

Anabolic steroid use is illegal and harmful. Anabolic steroids are a synthetic version of testosterone, the male sex hormone. Thus, anabolic steroids build muscle tissue bulking up the user, both male and female. The anabolic steroid user can also experience a deepening voice.

Anabolic steroid usage is linked to liver cancer, its use reduces sperm count, causes male and female sterility, increases early male pattern balding, stunts growth in adolescents, causes irritability, rage and mood swings, leading some to coin the term "roid –rage." Anabolic steroids also increase cholesterol and blood pressure, leaving users with an increased risk for heart attack and stroke.[6]

Anabolic steroids give athletes a definite physical advantage which is unfair to other competitors who "play by the rules."

It's hard enough being an adolescent. In order for children to make good decisions, form good friendships, and avoid risky behaviors, they need to steer clear of risk-filled activities that will affect their reasoning, decision-making ability and behavior. Furthermore, parents are advised to learn the warning signs of drug and alcohol abuse, including: being overly tired; having reduced interest in school, grades, friends and families; smelling alcohol or tobacco on the breath; other smells on clothing or hair; increased use of chewing gum before arriving home; red eyes; increased physical or sexual aggression; depression; emotional outbursts; sleeping and eating problems; acting in a threatening way; skipping school; finding unexplained rags soaked in solvents around the home or outside; observing unusual and unexplained stains on fingers and hands; or acts of theft or vandalism.

Safe sex

Safe sex is all about how to use someone with the least amount of *physical consequence*. Using others - even when trying to reduce its physical ends — is hardly admirable.

The definition of love is varied and loaded with different meanings for different people. Boys use *love* to get sex and girls use sex to get *love*. Neither arrives at *true love,* which never uses another to get anything.

Safe sex is a myth that needs to be debunked – the faster the better. Isn't it funny how society holds onto such myths despite being technologically advanced and scientific? Perhaps people think if they say it often enough, it will become reality.

Teens suffer greatly if they begin a sexual relationship; unfortunately most sexually active teens have multiple sexual relationships with each one taking its toll. Most teens will eventually break up with their current boyfriend or girlfriend. Breaking up is one of the most common causes for teen murders, suicides and depression according to Dr. Sheryl Feinstein. First, teens lack coping skills, communication skills and a solid core identity. Did you know that some experts suggest that a teen brain can only "stay" in love about 4 months? Adult brains can of course stay in love for a lifetime depending on the hedges they build and the care they take to grow their love relationship.

While many teens claim to be in love, they don't stay there because of brain development, maturation, sudden new interests and numerous other reasons. Obviously, combining sex with this premature state of brain development only serves to endanger teens.

Using a term commonly from the 1970s — *let's go all the way* — philosopher Dr. Ann Maloney offers teens a response to a boy or girl friend pressuring them into sexual relations. "Sure we can go all the way, after you have gone *all the way* to the altar." Marriage is the *only* time sex is safe, sex is good and sex expresses authentic love. Any other time, sex uses another to get something for oneself.

There is no such thing as safe sex if you are having sex with someone infected with an STD, AIDS or during the fertile time of a woman's cycle. All the clever one-liners which coined this myth will not change these facts: if you have sex with an infected person, you can also contract the same infection; if you are having sex during the fertile time, even using contraceptives, there is still a chance of pregnancy. No contraceptives work 100 percent of the time.

For years, it had been suggested that STDs would disappear or significantly decrease as safe sex practices were adopted and new treatments were found for bacterial and viral infections. This myth has been costly for the U.S. The medical and social communities continue promoting ineffective safe sex propaganda, and more and more incidences of STDs are being reported. A study released in 2008 by the Centers for Disease Control reveals 20 percent of American teenage girls have an STD.

Treatments for bacterial STDs, developed more than sixty years ago, promised to eradicate syphilis and gonorrhea. Yet U.S. rates for syphilis, gonorrhea and chlamydia are higher than ever, and new strains keep turning up.

Dr. Stephen Genuis writes in the *American Journal of Obstetrics and Gynecology*: "Health professionals, educators and policy makers have promoted strategies that focus on risk reducing barrier protection as well as disease management. The lack of impact on STD rates and the enormous personal and social consequences of these infections make it imperative that primary prevention strategies which focus on underlying problem behaviors become a focus of prevention problems." This explains that condom distribution programs have done little to reduce the spread of STDs. Society's risk reduction strategies are failing. Genuis' call to action is clear: focus on underlying problem *behaviors*.

The consequences of sexual relationships conducted outside of marriage are many.

HIV/AIDS

In the very same article, Dr. Genuis calls HIV/AIDs the most "complex problem facing humanity today." A 2004 report issued by the World Health Organization calls the infection the leading cause of death among fifteen to fifty-nine year olds worldwide and the second leading cause of serious sickness and disability in the world. It infects an estimated 14,000 people each day. AIDS is well known to be in Africa, Eastern Europe and Asia and the threat posed by this dire pandemic threatens developing countries'civil order, economies and infrastructures.

In "Managing the Sexually Transmitted Disease Pandemic: A Time For Reevaluation," Dr. Genuis writes: "Although clinical trials of HIV vaccines may offer hope for achieving some degree of protection from this virus in the future, testing is in the early stages and there is danger that a false sense of security will be engendered if individuals begin to believe that an effective vaccine is imminent."[7]

Allow me to restate this. There is no cure for HIV/AIDS. While there are combination drug treatments which prolong the lives of people living with the infection, there is no cure. The treatments that are available are quite expensive.

Human Papillomavirus (HPV)

The U.S. Centers for Disease Control estimates that 50 percent to 75 percent of sexually active men and women acquire HPV at some point in their lives. That makes HPV the most common sexually transmitted infection in the United States.

HPV is difficult to contain because it's transmissible in its very early stages, and is transmissible even when an infected person does not show any symptoms. Condoms cannot completely prevent the spread of HPV; what's worse, experts report that there's at least a 50 percent chance of HPV transmission with a single sexual encounter with an infected person.

While it's true HPV symptoms are treatable, most people don't realize this STD is incurable and is associated with genital cancer in both men and women. Additionally, HPV subtypes are directly known to cause cervical carcinoma — the most common cause of cancer-related deaths among women worldwide. HPV also has been implicated with cancer of the penis and anal area in men; HPV causes cervical, vaginal, and vulvar cancers in women; and causes head and neck tumors, oral, respiratory and esophageal cancers, non-melanoma skin and cutaneous cancers in both men and women.

HPV is transmissible through oral sex or any skin-to-skin, genital to genital contact. Considering how easily HPV is transmitted, Dr. Genuis called its containment a "significant challenge." Certain factors increase one's risk for acquiring HPV: promiscuous lifestyles, lack of circumcision in males, early age of first sexual intercourse, smoking, and use of oral contraceptives.

Although this STD is incurable, its secondary infections and diseases are treatable when timely and appropriate medical intervention occurs. In 2006, several vaccines against HPV were approved by the FDA and made available to young girls and women. The available vaccines are made up of virus-like particles, or VLPs, which resemble HPV types. The VLPs cause the immune system to generate neutralizing antibodies that bond to natural HPV viruses and block their entry into cells. Two vaccines were tested and proven to protect against four HPV types responsible for 70 percent of cervical cancers and 90 percent of genital warts.

The response to the HPV vaccine has been lukewarm for a variety of reasons: some want more information about the prevalence, transmission and consequences of HPV; some parents question the safety, degree of protection, and side effects of the vaccine; some hint the vaccine is painful compared with most vaccinations; some feel the cost of the vaccine is too high; some question the morality of vaccinating virginal girls against an STD (the vaccines are ineffective once first sexual intercourse has occurred); while others feel STD vaccines give a false sense of protection from disease and infections among women and men.

Herpes Simplex Virus (HSV)

The herpes simplex virus can lead to painful sores or ulcerations. One type of the virus, HSV Type 1, is what commonly causes cold sores in and around the mouth. Type 2 HSV is the sexually transmitted disease that leads to genital sores and skin lesions found on the thigh and buttocks. It is commonly known as genital herpes. Both types of virus can be spread through direct contact – even kissing. Also 15 percent to 25 percent of all genital herpes cases are caused by HSV Type 1, spread to the genital area.

Like HPV, transmission of HSV can occur even when the infected individual does not see or feel their sores.

HSV is a common infection in the United States according to the CDC, which reports that at least forty-five million people ages twelve and older, or one out of five adolescents and adults, have had a genital HSV infection. Additionally, between the late 1970s and the early 1990s, the number of Americans with genital herpes infection increased 30 percent.

Genital herpes is generally more painful for women than for men. Genital herpes cannot be cured although symptoms can be treated; once the virus is in a person, they will have it for life. Infected persons can normally experience five flare-ups in the first year alone. Flare-ups may involve the development of blisters, fever, itching, painful urination, swollen lymph nodes, pain in the legs, and tiredness. Periodic flare-ups can be expected thereafter, with future flare-ups coinciding with anxiety, emotional upset, onset of ovulation, or menstruation in women.

HSV increases the risk of acquiring other STDs such as HIV, due in part to ready transmission via open sores. HSV also seems to be a cofactor in having increased risk of developing cervical cancer. Mother to baby transmission is possible during childbirth, posing a significant health risk for the child. Herpes infection brings a woman a three-fold increased risk for miscarriage and premature labor. Also infected babies are at greater risk for irreversible brain damage or even death.

Chlamydia

One of the major causes of infertility among women is Chlamydia. The disease leads to tubal infertility, ectopic pregnancy, pelvic inflammatory disease (PID) and chronic pelvic pain. In fact, Chlamydia accounts for 20 percent to 50 percent of the PID cases annually. Unlike HPV and HSV, Chlamydia is a bacterial STD. It also has been found to contribute to the development of cervical cancer and other pelvic maladies.

While it's true Chlamydia can be treated and eradicated, it often is a symptom-less disease in its early stages, damaging internal structures before diagnosis occurs and treatment begins.

The CDC estimates 2.8 to 4 million Americans are infected with Chlamydia each year. Women who receive treatment for Chlamydia will become re-infected if their partners are not treated as well.

Babies also can become infected with Chlamydia when born to infected mothers. This puts them at high risk for developing pneumonia, perinatal death, and conjunctivitis.[8] In 1984, more than 300,000 infants died or were born with significant birth defects after they became infected with STDs transferred from their mothers.

Gonorrhea

Gonorrhea most commonly impacts the cervix and the fallopian tubes in women and the anterior portion of a man's urethra. Rectal areas may also be affected and, if the disease goes untreated, other areas of the body are susceptible. The infection causes a burning sensation in affected areas.

Vaginal discharge and/or slight urinary discomfort are early symptoms of this disease. Like Chlamydia, much of the damage done by an infection of Gonorrhea occurs before symptoms exacerbate to the point where a person seeks treatment. When Gonorrhea spreads to the uterus and fallopian tubes, or male sperm ducts, sterility occurs. Gonorrhea also increases an infected woman's risk for having an ectopic pregnancy. Gonorrhea is associated with increased cases of arthritis, heart disease, eye infection, blindness, meningitis and PID. Between 10 percent and 15 percent of PID cases are due to Gonorrhea.

Pregnant women infected with Gonorrhea are at increased risk for giving birth to low birth weight or premature infants. Also, infected infants can become blinded by the bacteria.

Nearly 20 percent of men infected with Gonorrhea will not have any symptoms; still, the disease will spread to infect the prostate or testicles. It also will continue to be transmitted to their sexual partners.

Hepatitis

The CDC defines Hepatitis as an inflammation of the liver. Viral Hepatitis is inflammation of the liver caused by a virus. In the United States, Hepatitis A (HAV), Hepatitis B (HBV) and Hepatitis C (HCV) are the most common types.

Hepatitis A is transmitted by putting something in the mouth that has been contaminated with the stool of a person with HAV. This type of transmission is called "fecal-oral" and is not generally considered a sexually transmitted disease. HAV can be passed through sexual contact, however. There is an available preventive vaccine for Hepatitis A.

Hepatitis B is spread when blood or other bodily fluids from an infected person enters the body of another person. HBV is readily transmitted through sexual intercourse and is widely recognized as a serious STD. This infection can be found in blood, semen, vaginal secretions and saliva. It can be passed onto a child born to an infected mother. It also is transmitted through shared needles.

There is a vaccine available to help prevent HBV; persons infected with the virus may recover with treatment, however they remain at risk to develop chronic liver problems and are at increased risk for cancer and even death.

Hepatitis C is transmitted by sharing needles, receiving an infected blood product, or being infected by non-sterile instruments used for body piercing, tattooing, or acupuncture. HCV also can be transferred from an infected mother to unborn child. Transmission is spread through blood. Sexual intercourse is not thought to be involved in the transmission of HCV unless blood is present. Blood could be present if there is a break in the skin, there is an open sore, or during female menstruation. There is no vaccine available for this disease.

Syphilis

Syphilis is passed from person to person through direct contact with a sore. Sores occur mainly on the external genitals, vagina, anus, or in the rectum, although they also may appear on the lips and in the mouth. Transmission of the organism occurs during vaginal, anal, or oral sex. Infected mothers can pass it to babies they are carrying. Syphilis cannot be spread through contact with toilet seats, doorknobs, swimming pools, hot tubs, bathtubs, shared clothing, or eating utensils. Many of the signs and symptoms of Syphilis are indistinguishable from other diseases.

Syphilis undergoes three stages when left untreated. During the first three weeks (stage one), the infected person develops a painless lesion in the genital area. This heals in a few weeks; roughly six weeks later, more skin lesions and flu-like symptoms appear. This is stage two. Stage two subsides in about three weeks and then disease enters the latent stage (stage three) without major complaints from the infected person. If Syphilis goes untreated, the infection will remain in the person and they may find themselves periodically bouncing back and forth between stage two and stage three.

Syphilis has the potential to cause serious damage to internal organs, including the brain, nerves, eyes, heart, blood vessels, liver, bones, and joints. This internal damage may show up many years later. Signs and symptoms of the late stage of Syphilis include difficulty coordinating muscle movements, paralysis, numbness, gradual blindness, and dementia. This damage may be serious enough to cause death.

Trichomoniasis (Trich or TV)

A very common sexually transmitted disease that affects both women and men, although symptoms are more common in women, is Trichomoniasis. Infection is caused by the single-celled protozoan parasite, *trichomonas vaginalis*. The vagina is the most common site of infection in women, and the urinary canal is the most common site of infection in men. The parasite is sexually transmitted however, the parasite can live outside of a body for several hours when protected by a moist environment, such as on sponges or wet towels. It is possible for a person to become infected by TV parasites after using these wet objects.

Most men with Trichomoniasis do not have signs or symptoms; however, some men may temporarily have an irritation inside the penis, mild discharge, or slight burning after urination or ejaculation. Men carry the organism in their urethra.

Some women have signs or symptoms of infection which include a frothy, yellow-green vaginal discharge with a strong odor. The infection also may cause discomfort during intercourse and urination, as well as irritation and itching of the female genital area. In rare cases, lower abdominal pain can occur. Symptoms usually appear in women within five to twenty-eight days of exposure. Trichomoniasis can usually be cured with medication.

The CDC estimates 3 million new cases of TV are diagnosed annually.

Vaginitis

Vaginitis symptoms are similar to those from Trichomoniasis. Bacterial Vaginosis (BV-Candidiasis) is the name of a condition in women where the normal balance of bacteria in the vagina is disrupted and replaced by an overgrowth of certain bacteria. Candidiasis is normally accompanied by a clumpy, white discharge, odor, pain, itching, or burning. The CDC is unclear what role sexual activity plays in the development of BV, although women who have never had sexual intercourse are rarely affected. BV is transmissible through sexual intercourse. The infection is not normally dangerous but can be problematic in pregnant women. It also can cause Pelvic Inflammatory Disease (PID). BV can be a stubborn infection despite being treatable with antibiotics.

Women who are pregnant, have increased blood sugar levels, regularly use antibiotics, use the birth control pill, or have poor hygiene during bathroom visits, have increased risk for developing candidiasis.

Women are cautioned to always wipe from front to back (not vice versa) after going to the bathroom; this will help prevent contaminating the urinary tract or vagina with fecal matter. Mothers should begin practicing proper wiping technique when changing diapers of infant daughters and instruct their daughters the same as they toilet train.

Pediculosis Pubis (Pubic Lice)

Also called "crabs," Pubic Lice are one of three types of crabs - parasitic insects found on humans. These bothersome creatures infest the genital areas of humans and cause intense itching and irritation of that area; Pubic Lice also has been found on the scalp, eyelashes, and under the arms. Pubic Lice is most frequently transmitted through direct contact with the genitals of an infected person. Infestation in a young child or teenager may indicate sexual activity or sexual abuse. Pubic Lice is not the same as Head Lice but like Head Lice, it is not considered dangerous and can be treated. Pubic Lice infestations increase during the winter months.

Molluscum Contagiosum

Molluscum Contagiosum is caused by a virus which leads to a mild skin disease. The virus affects only the outer layers of skin and does not circulate throughout the body in healthy people. It causes small white, pink, or flesh-colored raised bumps or growths with a dimple or pit in the center. The benign tumors are usually smooth and firm. Molluscum Contagiosum is transmitted through touch, both sexual and non-sexual touch; only since the late 1970s has it been regarded as a sexually transmitted disease. The virus lives only in the skin and once the growths are gone, the virus cannot spread. The benign tumors can be removed either by surgery or with chemicals – the process can be easy or difficult depending on tumor number and size.

Scabies

Scabies is a parasitic infestation of the skin. It causes pimple-like irritations or rash, especially in the webbing between fingers, in skin folds on the wrist, elbow, knee, penis, breast or shoulder blades. Scabies causes intense itching.

Scabies is transmitted through direct *prolonged* contact with the skin of an infested person. A hug or handshake does not provide sufficient skin-to-skin contact to spread Scabies. Infestation is easily spread to sexual partners but can also occur by sharing bed clothes or under garments with an infected person. Scabies is treated topically.

The cost of sexual freedom

The afflictions listed above are the most common sexually transmitted diseases now being reported in the United States. They are not, however, the only diseases that spread through sexual contact. Others include: Cytomegalovirus (a danger to newborns); Amebiasis (which causes intestinal problems); Giardiasins (a parasitic infection); Group B Beta Hemolytic Streptococcal Infection (a danger to newborns); Mycoplasma infection (associated with infertility and spontaneous abortions); Shigella and Salmonella; Bacterial Infection; and Epstein Barr virus. Every year, more organisms are added to the list of those that are transmitted through sexual contact.

Yet people continue to take huge risks to seek out illicit sexual pleasure. Why? Psychologists offer some insights:

• Some people pursue sex to assuage pre-sexual needs such as to account for any emotional trauma suffered from lack of parental participation.

• Teenagers often time the onset of sexual activity to correspond with that of their peers.

• Television and movies have a powerful influence over teenagers' sexual attitudes, values and beliefs.

• Readily available "adult" material affects the sexual attitudes of young viewers.

• The average eighteen-year-old spends more time in front of the television or on line than in a classroom.

• Peer-to-peer pornography delivered via email is the primary way teens are exposed to sexually explicit material. Cellphones are used to send explicit pictures to others as well.

• Risky sexual activity frequently accompanies the use of mood-altering drugs, especially alcohol.

• Once a teenager becomes sexually active, they are more likely to engage in subsequent sexual relationships.

Helping teenagers equip themselves to navigate a culture preoccupied with sex is a parents' greatest challenge. After briefing yourself on all the diseases that can be spread through sexual contact, you're sure to see that pre-marital and extra-marital sex is risky business indeed! What may on the surface seem like an innocent encounter with one partner is in fact an encounter with everyone with whom that person has had sexual contact in their past.

Contraceptives and condoms don't provide protection from the diseases outlined above. There's no way to engage in "casual" sex and believe you can stay safe. Safe sex isn't just a myth; it's an out and out lie!

STD's other effects

Typically, physicians focus their treatments on the physical symptoms endured by those who've contracted a sexually transmitted disease. Yet those who suffer infections such as the ones listed above also suffer psychological damage. Individuals who contract an STD may experience increased feelings of anger, depression, isolation, rejection or guilt, which may impact them long term.

As Dr. Genuis stated earlier, condoms as barriers provide little protection from the skin-to-skin, or sore-to-sore transmissions. Anyone who believes there are ways to reduce their risk by using condoms or by changing their position is opening themselves up for a horrible consequence.

Here are more alarming trends from the last 35 years, compiled from the CDC and other sources and published in *Teen Reality Check* by Dr. Genuis:

- The percentage of teens involved in sexual activity has nearly doubled.
- The average age that teens begin having sex has decreased.
- Physicians are seeing more twelve to thirteen year olds who are sexually active.
- The average number of sexual partners during the teen years has increased, further increasing the risk they'll contract an STD.
- Sex with high risk partners has increased.
- Illegal drug use in teens has escalated.
- Rates of infection with STDs has increased substantially.
- Teen pregnancy rates are up.

Red flags should go up as we learn that not everyone discloses to their sexual partner(s) the fact that they carry an STD. One study found that peoples' willingness to disclose the presence of an STD was dependent "on the level of intimacy they felt they had with their sexual partner." In fact, from 42 percent to 89 percent of the people surveyed may or may not disclose their STD depending on certain factors.[9] This translates to a whole lot of deception, with new infections occurring rapidly. Furthermore, the reason why people do or don't disclose their STD can best be chalked up to selfishness. Reasons many people gave for failing to disclose their STD included: fear of discrimination, fear that the relationship would dissolve, fear of losing financial support, emotional protection, self protection, and the concealment of one's homosexuality.[10]

The same study revealed: "Only 52 percent of participants agreed with the statement: *they must tell all sexual partners about their HPV*; a full one third, or 33 percent of the respondents, *didn't feel it was necessary* to disclose their infection or were not sure about the need to tell their sexual partner about having HPV; and 58 percent said they must disclose their HPV status if they had an obvious reoccurrence. Even people who understood the consequences of their STD *did not show any greater obligation* to inform their sexual partner about their STD! [11]

This sense of entitlement for pleasure, regardless of another's well-being, is troublesome. It demonstrates the seriousness of why it is wrong to use another human being as an object for our own pleasure — in the boldest of ways. It also demonstrates Pope John Paul II was right when he said that using another reduces the other to an object, by treating others in this way we reduce our ability to grow in our capacity to love authentically.

Whether you homeschool your children, send them to a private or religious school, or educate them through a large public school, perhaps one that doles out free contraceptives, the responsibility to teach your children Christian values and morals sits on your shoulders. Society believes it's inevitable that your children will become sexually active so it focuses on "safety education." But you know your child better than anybody can. You also know that "safety" is a false notion when it comes to pre-marital or extra-marital sex. Sex, as it's promoted these days in society, is fraught with consequences. Most are quite serious. Some can be deadly. Teenagers need to be educated about what can happen to them when they engage in "risky" behaviors.

But more than that, you are charged with the responsibility to pass your faith along to your children and help them grow closer to God. Help your teenager understand that chastity is God's gift to them. More than helping them avoid those "bad things" that come from immorality, help them to embrace the "good" that follows obedience. If you speak the truth to them often, then let them see you living it in your own marriage – they'll get it. And if your family is really blessed, they might even pass this truth along to some of their teenaged friends! ❦

chapter five

Eating Right: A Challenge for Teens

Nutrition affects our general and overall health status; there are other factors that affect our health as well but our individual nutritional status is often within our control. In other words, how healthy we *are* and even how healthy we will be *long term* is in part determined by what we eat, how much we eat, and even when we eat.

Parents, take notice about this bit of research. It has been confirmed that regular *family dinners* discourage teen girls from developing risky eating habits. Furthermore, one study showed when teen girls ate at least five meals per week with their families, they were less likely to engage in risky habits such as binge eating, chronic dieting, self induced vomiting, and diet pill use.[1]

Notice the ever-present and important link between healthy families and healthy teens: togetherness and connectedness. Unhealthy families and unhealthy teens with behavioral problems, including unsafe eating disorders equals disconnectedness. Family dinners are more than a "quaint slice of American life," to quote one writer. They discourage teen girls from developing risky eating habits.

Look around at your local fast food restaurant and what do you see? Teens eating out with friends. I continue to be amazed by how many teens are left to their own wiles for breakfast, lunch and supper. My own children often tell me about friends from school who go without lunch or breakfast. Feeding our children has gone institutional as schools have now added breakfast to the menu. Not too long ago, feeding children breakfast was the duty and responsibility of parents. In fact, years ago, parents who let their children go unfed routinely had to face social workers who threatened removal of their children. At the very least, these parents who shirked their duties faced the disdain of other parents.

No matter how busy a family is, schedules can be adjusted so parents and children can eat together — especially dinner. I recall a comment from our daughter-in-law who remembered, while she dated our son, how we always adjusted dinner schedules so all of us could share at least one meal together per day. It didn't matter whether they were in school, had games after school, or my husband worked late. We made dinner time sacred, even though the actual time varied some days by many hours. We thought every family did the same thing and it wasn't until my daughter-in-law's comment that I learned what we did was uncommon.

Thus, one key to healthy eating is establishing healthy eating habits. These are set early and primarily influenced by parents. If regular evening meals aren't shared in your family, research shows you should perhaps reconsider – the health of everyone in your family hinges on it. Setting family nutrition goals is primarily the parents' responsibility. Again, teens do what they see — if the family is eating a balanced meal together they will see and learn healthy eating habits. And, they will likely imitate them. If you regularly eat well-balanced meals, your teens will likely have already learned these eating habits as well.

Recall when your teenager was a baby; you either bottle-fed or breastfed him. He appeared to grow and thrive on this *single food source* probably until the age of around six months. None of us would be very healthy if we only ate one food source every meal, every day and every year of our life. Yet it was possible when we were infants; that was only possible because the "formula" is composed of multiple vitamins, minerals, and other necessary food nutrients. Better yet was breast milk, which contains more "necessary" ingredients than infant formula — in fact it contains more than 200 more natural ingredients than infant formula. Furthermore, research demonstrates that breastfed babies are smarter and healthier than bottle-fed babies. This example clearly shows how *what we eat affects* our overall health and welfare, both when we eat it, and in the future.

Thus it is important young children eat healthily once weaned from the breast. They must eat a variety of foods in order to obtain all the necessary nutrients including minerals and vitamins found in a variety of foods. In order for families to eat healthily, parents must establish key food habits and preferences. For instance, keep only healthy foods in the kitchen; in refrigerators, on pantry shelves, and in the freezer. These include storing up on a wide variety of fruits, vegetables, yogurt, cheese, and other milk products, along with beans and whole grains such as oats, brown rice, whole wheat cereal and breads. It also means not stocking "junk goods" such as chips, store-bought treats or snacks, soda-pop, juice, candy, and processed frozen foods. Also, avoid most fast food meals; "fast" food is higher in fats, salts and calories than most home-cooked meals, leaving you dissatisfied and looking for snacks or other foods not long after consuming them. By eating a variety of foods, you'll gain the most nutrients; when limiting variety, you severely limit your intake of key nutrients.

The government and others have established food pyramids which help families learn how much of each food groups a person should eat on any given day. We are instructed to eat from all food groups each meal, each day. For instance the My Pyramid developed by the U.S. Department of Agriculture shows how many grains, vegetables, fruits, fats, dairy, and meats, beans, fish or poultry are to be consumed each day. My Pyramid suggests that teen girls need at least two cups of fruit daily. Fruit juices do not substitute for fresh or frozen or canned fruits. Choosing a variety of fruits is important. Furthermore, My Pyramid suggests eating darker, green vegetables than the basic orange or yellow vegetables. Teens need two-and-a-half cups of vegetables per day.

Teen girls are encouraged to consume at least 1,300 mg of Calcium every day (this exceeds the 1,000 mg Calcium recommended for adults). To take in this much calcium, teen girls should be drinking milk and eating a variety of foods that are high in calcium such as other low-fat dairy products along with vegetables rich in calcium. Teens should be eating grains and proteins as well, although whole grains are preferred. Lean meats and poultry are preferred to high-fat meats. And, let's not forget beans, nuts and seeds, which all contribute to the protein count.

Fat free diets can be problematic. Here's why: Even if you cut fat from your diet, you can still gain weight if you consume more calories than are used up in energy output. When considering fat intake, what is important is the type of fats consumed. Trans fats are particularly bad for long term health and are found in most pre-prepackaged, processed foods and snacks. Saturated and trans fats are nicknamed "bad fats" because they increase "bad" cholesterol in the blood stream. The "good" fats, meanwhile, include mono- and poly-unsaturated fats; they are good because they do not increase bad cholesterol levels in the body. Good fats include olive oil, canola oil, and oils found naturally in foods such as avocados, fish and nuts.

Vegetarian diets – whether lacto-ovo (consumes eggs and milk but not meats) and vegan (consumes no form of animal product) — can be problematic for anyone who is not properly trained to manage them. Vegan/ vegetarian diets are especially problematic for teens who are still developing, growing and maturing. It's not uncommon for vegans who manage their own diets to not get enough Vitamin B12, Calcium, Iron, Zinc and Protein. Parents of vegetarian teens ought to provide their teen access to a nutritionist who can advise them of their eating plans.

Sometimes, it seems the emphasis for nutrition focuses more on young women than on young men. This is unfortunate, but one explanation is the fact that someday a young woman will likely become a mother. Her health status and nutritional state both *before* and *during* pregnancy determine her own future health and ability to assume her tasks with an appropriate energy once she becomes a mother. Her health also affects the development of her child. Consider how a woman's nutritional status may have a negative consequence on her unborn child, or even herself, if she enters a pregnancy under-nourished. A woman's pre-pregnancy nutritional stores are in part established during her teenage years, set by established habits and preferences – good and bad.

Eating disorders

The USDA's My Pyramid suggests teen girls need 2,000 calories per day; active girls and boys will need more. But for many teens, consuming calories is akin to taking poison. For these teens, an eating disorder is likely at play.

Two eating disorders that parents need to monitor include anorexia and bulimia. Both eating disorders are thought to present themselves due to a combination of biological, psychological and socio-cultural factors.

Studies suggest that between 1 percent and 10 percent of American girls and women have anorexia; 1 percent to 3 percent of girls and women experience bulimia. (Men and boys are significantly less effected by these disorders.) Both eating disorders are serious problems and warrant parental action.

Identified risk factors for having anorexia or bulimia include: a heavy focus on dieting, the onset of puberty combined with unhappiness with body shape; having a poor body image; receiving increased criticism or comments from others about weight or body shape; making difficult transitions which cause emotional distress; participating in sports; and participating in dance or modeling – two activities especially tied to an increased risk of having an eating disorder. Coaches and parents are advised not to suggest weight loss to child athletes.

Furthermore, fashion magazines and popular media promote ultra thinness as an ideal to which teen girls will aspire. For decades, young women have linked popularity and success to being ultra-thin. Think of model Twiggy from the 1960s or, more recently, Kate Moss.

The Mayo Clinic suggests the following warning signs for parents to be aware of so they can monitor and stay ahead of any emerging eating problems. Risky Eating Red Flags include: regularly skipping meals; making excuses for not eating; eating only low fat or low calorie foods; cutting food into tiny pieces; spitting food out after chewing; weighing food; refusing to eat meals they prepared for someone else; repeated weighing of oneself; frequent checking in mirror for flaws; wearing baggy or layered clothing; complaining excessively of being fat; constant dieting; going to the bathroom after eating, and hoarding food.

Healthy weight

Teens often misunderstand "healthy" weights. Girls often want to be thinner than they are. We previously discussed eating disorders associated with having a poor body image. Assessing one's weight should be done by a medical doctor, who will use a Body Mass Index (BMI) chart to assess proper body weight to height.

If a teen needs to lose weight, he or she will simply be encouraged to change food choices and eating habits and to increase daily activity or exercise. All teens should get at least 60 minutes of exercise per day and most won't need to restrict their food intake to actively lose weight unless they eat a lot of junk food. Too many teens think if they skimp on the main course of a meal, they can reserve calories for dessert. This is an unhealthy choice with consequences since the intake of nutritious minerals, vitamins, and other nutrients is cut short by this action.

The U.S. government advises teens not to skip meals or eat only bread and water at a meal. Teens also should not take diet pills or dietary supplements or assume quick weight loss programs or diets. These can be dangerous and can cause gallstones, hair loss, fatigue and diarrhea.[2]

A healthy diet includes a variety of foods in healthy serving sizes. Parents can oversee this when they purchase the food, cook it and sit down with their children to eat at the family table. The old saying went: the family that prays together stays together. I think the contemporary version of this could go something like this: the family that eats together is healthier and happier. ❦

chapter six

Abortion: Society's Litmus Test

It seems abortion has morphed from a moral issue to a political one; it's now most often viewed as a litmus test in judicial appointments and congressional races. Those who oppose abortion are neatly labeled "conservative" while those who line up in support of abortion are pegged "liberal." Those who don't fit neatly in either camp are often the people who say they're "personally opposed" to abortion but are reluctant to impose their beliefs on others. As a result, abortion has become a topic ordinary people are reluctant to address, debate, or even think about. Yet while abortion wins and losses are tallied between political parties or ignored by the politically ambivalent, innocent babies continue to die.

At least two generations, those born after Roe vs. Wade legalized abortion nationwide, have been mostly conditioned to view abortion as a legal matter best debated in the halls of Congress or decided by the nine judges of the Supreme Court. The ambivalent among us don't have the stomach to judge others when it comes to abortion. "I would never do it but I can't judge others," has become the mantra for a societal tragedy of epic proportions. What is wrong with a society that can't put personal conviction toward reversing a moral crisis? Everything!

The Guttmacher Institute, a nonprofit organization that focuses on reproductive policy and health issues, reports that more than 1.2 million babies were aborted in 2003. In the same year, the CDC reported nearly 4.1 million live births. It's not hard to see these figures and conclude that nearly 24 percent of all pregnancies end in abortion. That's nearly one baby killed for every four who are born. While statistics may be viewed by some as cold, that one is downright chilling!

Is it any wonder people are reluctant to bring such a statistic to the dinner table or open a discussion on the ratio of abortion to live births when visiting with friends over coffee? With so few willing to fight for the voiceless, how will Americans come to view abortion as more than a mere political volleyball?

Maybe things would be different if we could attach a face to this nation's abortion statistics. Perhaps, if only we could give abortion a name, attitudes might begin to change.

Meet Deborah

In the fall of 2006, I was a guest on EWTN *Live*, a television interview program hosted by Fr. Mitch Pacwa, in order to discuss natural family planning. The interview went well and, as expected, abortion never entered into our discussion. Before my return flight home the next morning, I attended morning Mass presided over by Fr. Frank Pavone, one of the most prominent pro-life warriors engaged in the battle to end abortion. When the service ended, Fr. Pavone invited us to stay in the church to participate in a prayer service for Deborah, who was soon to be buried at the cemetery at Our Lady of the Angels Monastery in Hanceville, Alabama. (Mother Angelica resides at this monastery.)

As I watched a tiny casket being carried onto the altar, I decided to stay and participate in the service. When the casket was opened, I saw Deborah – an 18-week fetus, a victim of abortion. Deborah had been aborted a week earlier at a clinic in the Washington D.C. area. Her body was taken to the local coroner and then transferred to Alabama by a pro-life group so she could be given a funeral.

As I listened to the service, I learned Deborah's abortion had been performed through the use of prostaglandins, drugs that induce violent contractions; her small body was then pulled from her mother's uterus with forceps. (Abortion methods are discussed later in this chapter.) Prostaglandins are not commonly used to perform abortions because there is an increased risk of the fetus being delivered alive.

I studied Deborah. She was about 12 inches long and eerily resembled a friend's preemie who had been born at just 20 weeks gestation and was now doing well. Her arms, legs and chest were bruised and black from the pressure of the forceps, yet her tiny face and head remained perfectly intact and was still beautifully pink as one might expect from a babe newly emerged from the womb. Her small body was completely intact. Her little legs were tucked up to her chest yet her toes and fingers were wide-spread apart, as if her nervous system had been reacting to pain or trauma just before her life ended. She had long feet and graceful, slender fingers. She didn't have any hair on her head and probably would've been a "baldy" as my daughters had been. Deborah looked like any other perfect little baby except she was bruised. And she was dead.

As I sat there praying for Deborah, I wondered if her mother saw her after the abortion. I wondered what had happened to her mother to lead her to choose this horrible death for her child. I wondered how long it would take for her mother to fill with regret over Deborah's abortion. I wondered about the doctor who performed this abortion and probably hundreds of others. Would Deborah ever affect him or her the way she affected me? And, I cried, as did every other person attending the service that day. I cried with strangers. I wept for Deborah, the 18-week fetus who will forever be the face I attach to this horrible thing called abortion.

First, there was Angela

More than a dozen years earlier, I met a girl I'll call Angela. She lived with a guardian because her mother had died and her father wasn't interested in raising her. At 15, Angela got pregnant. Angela's guardian had arranged for the girl to have an abortion at the Planned Parenthood clinic operating in my neighborhood. I learned about Angela after her grandmother, who was opposed to abortion, called me for help.

My first attempt to help led me to a pro-life organization who gathered some pro-life literature for me to give Angela. Unfortunately, her guardian intercepted the material before Angela could see it. Next, I called the clinic on the day of the scheduled abortion to try to talk her out of staying. The clinic would neither confirm nor deny Angela's presence there. I was placed on hold for a lengthy period of time but never connected with Angela. Angela proceeded with the abortion and celebrated that same evening with a party thrown by her guardian.

The next day, Angela's grandmother called me again. The police had come to her door, she said, with a warrant for my arrest which they asked her to sign. The warrant said I was being charged with stalking Angela. Fortunately for me and my family, the grandmother refused to sign the arrest warrant.

In the years following her abortion, her grandmother would tell me about Angela's substance abuse, how she bounced from one troubled relationship to another, and even attempted suicide. Only recently has Angela been able to recover from this horrible "choice" and turn her life around.

Anybody's daughter; one more lost child

Two years after my encounter with Angela, my husband and I were driving past that same neighborhood Planned Parenthood clinic when something startling caught our attention. There was an ambulance in the Clinic's parking lot which told us somebody's abortion had gotten complicated. One misguided young woman who turned to Planned Parenthood to fix her problem was now discovering her plans had gone even more horribly awry.

It's this instance that I point to as a reminder that one abortion creates two victims: the mother within whose body these violent acts occur, and the innocent baby who is robbed of God's most precious gift — life!

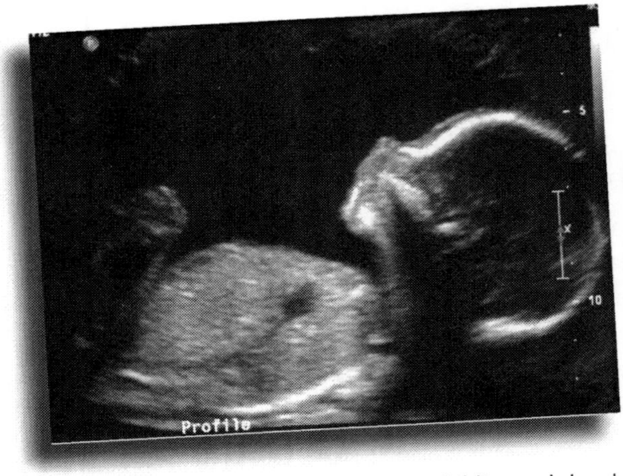

Whenever I hear the word abortion being bandied about by politicians I think about Deborah, Angela, and the girl in the ambulance. They are my touchstones on the issue that's all too often dismissed as a legal matter, a medical issue, a matter of personal privacy...choice. Abortion always has been and always will remain an issue of morals. When

At 18 weeks gestation, this developing child's vocal chords are formed and he can now go through the motions of crying, although without air, he won't make a sound. This is the same gestational age at which Deborah was aborted as described on page 88.

a child is aborted, his or her life ends. This is not a debatable point, which may be why so many are reluctant to debate abortion on this, its most troubling facet.

People have talked to me and tried to sway me over to the pro-choice side but always, my heart remains steadfast, my memory, with Deborah in her casket in Alabama.

The arguments

People who support abortion will argue its merits as if it were a panacea for all the problems facing today's women. Their arguments include the procedure's safety in comparison with carrying a child to term, how women who choose abortion may be lifted out of poverty, how rape victims shouldn't be forced to endure pregnancy after suffering a violent attack, how the government has no business legislating women's bodies, or how access to abortion instills gender equity.

I would argue that all of these arguments are built upon flawed logic and skewed statistics. Let's look at the facts:

Is abortion really saving lives?

In the early 1970s, it was argued that women needed legal access to abortions because pregnancy put women's lives at risk. In the 1990s, the Kaiser Family Foundation published statistics gathered from the U.S. Centers for Disease Control that touted abortion as one of the safest surgical procedures in the United States, with 0.6 deaths per 100,000 abortions. By comparison, the risk of maternal death from childbirth was 6.7 per 100,000 deliveries.[1]

But it's easy to see through such numbers. How many deaths really occur per 100,000 abortions? Using the same Kaiser Foundation statistics, the answer is: 100,000 babies and 0.6 mothers. Clearly, the abortion procedure was not a safe one for the majority of persons involved if you count the unborn as persons!

It was also argued in the 1970s that failing to legalize abortion would put some 5,000 to 10,000 abortion-seeking women at risk for death because so-called, "coat hanger," or self-induced abortions were their only alternative.

Yet, according to a 1960 report in the *American Journal of Public Health* referenced by Candace Crandall in *The Cost of Choice*, prior to the Roe vs. Wade decision, nine out of ten illegal abortions had indeed been performed by a licensed physician, not in some back alley by a friend of a friend. Moreover, as surgical techniques improved and antibiotic use became more prevalent during the 1960s, the number of deaths attributed to illegal abortions fell from 159 in 1966 to forty-one by 1972.

But death is not the only consequence to abortion.

A study conducted in the late 1970s by the Population Council reveals that roughly 12 percent of women who had an abortion reported other complications. The number was lower for women who aborted during the first trimester and much higher for those who aborted later in the pregnancy. About half the women who reported complications suffered serious ones, such as cardiac arrest, convulsions, endotoxic shock, hemorrhage, thrombophlebitis, pulmonary embolism, or damage to bladder, ureter or intestines.[2]

Some studies also link abortion to as much as a 30 percent increased risk for developing breast cancer. Three states – Minnesota, Mississippi and Texas – mandate counseling about the increased risk of breast cancer linked to abortion.

Finally, the argument against coat hanger abortions might lead to the belief that all abortions performed prior to 1973 were illegal. Data compiled by W. Robert Johnston and published in a document titled *Historical Abortion Statistics for the United States*, shows that between 1926 and 1972, 1.34 million legal abortions were performed in the United States.[3] Remember, Roe vs. Wade "legalized" abortion nationwide; the procedure was legal in many states prior to this landmark Supreme Court decision.

With legal abortions available in many parts of the country prior to 1973, the image of "back alley" abortions should only be considered a marketing tool to engender fear among women and to advance the pro-choice agenda.

Today, the abortion rate stands at around 20 percent. This rate translates into one out of every five pregnancies ending in abortion. Abortion certainly is not saving these babies lives. Instead, it generates two victims: the child who was killed and the mother who bears the spiritual, psychological, and physical loss. This doesn't include the emotionally traumatized men: the fathers not given a voice or the fathers who forced the abortion by threatening abandonment or the withholding of financial assistance. Men suffer as well.

Allow me to share my perspective on the issue of abortion chosen for reasons of fetal health. I have been changed by each of my seven children as they are each unique persons. My youngest child has Down Syndrome and she is a gift equal to her brothers and sisters. In the entire city of St. Paul, Minnesota, where I live, there are only three other children with Down Syndrome her age within the public school system, despite the fact that the rate for this diagnosis is generally one out of one hundred.

So, where are all the others like her? According to a specialist from the Mayo Clinic, the vast majority of fetuses who test positively for deformities such as Down Syndrome are now aborted.

My daughter is a bright, loving individual; how sad that some children who could have been her friends were not given the chance to prove their worth because a diagnosis led to fear, which led to abortion.

"With God all things are possible — fear not!"

Is abortion a panacea for rape victims?

Thirty-plus years since abortion was legalized nationwide, we still hear its advocates tout abortion as rightful justice for victims of rape and incest. Let's look at the statistics.

In a 2003 report detailing abortion statistics, only 4.5 percent of women surveyed cited health or other reasons for seeking an abortion.[4]

Of all study participants: 25.5 percent chose abortion to postpone childbearing; 7.9 percent chose abortion because they didn't want any more children; 21.3 percent said they could not afford a baby; 10.8 percent said the child would disrupt education or a job; 14.1 percent had relationship problems or had a partner who did not support the pregnancy; and 12.2 percent said they were too young or said their parents did not support the pregnancy. That leaves the remaining 4.5 percent choosing abortion for reasons of fetal health, maternal health, or other (2.1 percent).

In other words, 95.5 percent of all abortions were performed as birth control because some other force in these women's lives conflicted with the pregnancy – it was either the wrong time, or they had the wrong bank account balance, or they worked at the wrong job, or it was the wrong time or with the wrong partner, etc. Forty-eight percent of these abortions occurred solely because of timing issues.

It's important to know that the overall rate of pregnancy from having normal "unprotected" sexual intercourse between all fertile persons is about 3 percent. The typical pregnancy rate filtered through the rate of reported rapes in the United States theoretically could result in 9,000 to 10,000 pregnancies per year.[5] However, trauma often stifles ovulation

Gianna Beretta Molla

Women of faith can take example from the life of this newly canonized woman: Gianna Beretta Molla (1922-1962) especially if faced with this dreadful choice: Her own life or that of her baby?

Dr. Gianna Molla, born in Milan, Italy, in 1922, was said to be gifted with intelligence and faith, sometimes a rare combination. After earning her medical degree in 1949, specializing in pediatrics and surgery, she opened a medical clinic in Mesero, Italy. Dr. Gianna viewed her work as a mission by which she could care for women, babies, the elderly and the poor. Gianna Beretta married Pietro Molla in 1955, several years after opening her clinic. She was excited to marry Pietro and anxious to "form a truly Christian family." She gave birth to three children in the 1950's: Pierluigi (1956), Mariolona (1957) and Laura (1959). The Vatican reports that she "synchronized the duties and responsibilities of being a wife, a mother and a doctor with passion and incredible faith."

In September 1961 when Gianna was two months pregnant, doctors discovered a cancerous fibroma in her uterus. Gianna chose to save the life of her baby over her own by avoiding chemotherapy and surgery, which would harm the developing fetus. On the morning of April 21, 1962 Gianna gave birth to Gianna Emmanuela insisting that: "If you must decide between me and the child, do not hesitate, choose the child. I insist on it. Save him (her)." Despite all efforts and treatments to save mother and child, and reduce her pain, nothing worked for Gianna. At thirty-nine years old, Gianna Berretta died on April 28, 1962 while chanting: "Jesus I love you." Gianna Emmanuela lived.

On September 23, 1973, Pope Paul VI stated that Blessed Gianna was: "a young mother from the diocese of Milan, who, to give life to her daughter, sacrificed her own with conscious immolation." Immolation is defined as a sacrifice; in this case the Pope clearly defined Gianna's sacrifice as Christ-like referring to His own sacrifice on Calvary and in the Eucharist for the sake of our lives. Gianna Beretta Molla was beatified by Pope John Paul II on April 24, 1994 during the International Year of the Family.

A complimentary St. Gianna prayer card can be obtained online by visiting www.FortifyingFamiliesofFaith.com.

rendering rape victims infertile or temporarily sterile. Another factor is the rapist himself; he may be sterile or may fail to ejaculate "effectively" during the attack.

In 1971, the *Journal of the American Medical Association* documented 4,500 medically treated rape cases over a ten-year period in Minneapolis and St. Paul, Minnesota. In these cases, not one pregnancy resulted from these attacks.[6] Not one.

Nationally, in 2004, there were 0.3 rapes per 1,000 women compared to 2.8 rapes per 1,000 women in 1979, further devaluing the argument that legal abortion is necessary for women in case of rape.[7]

The bottom line is, even a child conceived through a horrible attack is a child of God, made in His image and likeness and thus should be guaranteed the same opportunity at life as a child conceived in a loving marriage.

Because of twenty-first century advances in medical technology, abortions performed to save the life of a mother are practically non-existent and thus have no legitimacy as a rallying cry for the pro-choice movement. Furthermore, mothers facing a tragic course of pregnancy may opt to give their babies the primary chance and herself only a secondary chance at life. A good example of this comes to us by way of one woman named Gianna Beretta Molla. (See opposite page.)

What about the economic impact?

Thirty years ago, abortion supporters claimed abortion would end illegitimacy. It has not.

More babies are born "out of wedlock" today than ever before. In his book, *Who We Are Now,* Sam Roberts reveals that in the fiscal year that ended in June 2002, one in three babies were born to single mothers – nine in ten of those were born to teenagers.

The number of children living in households headed by women is on the rise too. For white children the number is roughly 21 percent today, up from 9 percent in 1970; for black children, the statistics reveal 54 percent of children live in households headed by women, up from 33 percent in 1970.[8]

Roberts also reports the results of a Children's Defense Fund study that found nearly 700,000 black children were living in extreme poverty.[9]

Today, traditional families, defined as children living with both a mother and a father, represent only 68 percent of households in America, down from 87 percent in 1970.[10]

Thirty-plus years of legalized abortion have done nothing to improve the lives of millions of American children – or their mothers. And, it's done nothing to improve marriage and family life.

What about gender equity?

Since the equal rights movement began in the 1960s, women have been led to believe that equality to men ought to be their ultimate goal. The easiest way to achieve this equality, of course, is in the marketplace as a wage earner. The reality for women who seek equality through the generation of income, however, is that once a child enters the picture, a woman will most often elect to sacrifice income in order to become a caregiver. By guaranteeing a woman access to abortion, therefore, abortion is said to guarantee gender equity for women because it eliminates (by a woman's choice) the necessity of following a pregnancy to its natural conclusion.

But women have value and dignity because of their humanity, not because of their gender and certainly not because of their earning potential. Employment doesn't alter the fact that women are feminine and different from men and it doesn't alter the fact that women's bodies carry babies and men's cannot.

Employment may be able to equalize the genders on payday, but it certainly can't equalize the roles faced in parenting, especially when couples are establishing their family.

Men and women, instead of focusing on the size of their paychecks which has to do with their relationship to the outside world, ought to focus on cooperating with each other for the benefit of their shared household. Such cooperation has the potential to open new opportunities for both of them to enrich their lives without regard to "equity" issues. Cooperation between parents gives them an opportunity to build each other up rather than to exploit one another. Parenting with love and cooperation between spouses becomes one more opportunity for both to help build the kingdom of God here on earth.

So although some argue that abortion enables women to level the economic playing field, in reality it just opens them up to a gender war neither can emerge from victoriously.

The role of government

What is the role of government and should it be legislating activities related to our persons?

Some argue that our constitutional freedoms should be extended to reproductive freedom meaning they advocate for reproductive autonomy – one person decides. But it takes two people to create a third (along with God) so the decision to end a pregnancy cannot rest with one person alone.

Additionally, laws cannot alter fundamental human biology. The U.S. government cannot protect a person who chooses to have unlimited sex from suffering consequence anymore than it can protect such sexually active people from contracting STDs, for instance. Isn't that one of many consequences, in addition to pregnancy, from engaging in casual sex?

Translate this logic to other areas of life. Can the government, which guarantees our freedom, protect us from getting fat if we eat too many sweets? Can it protect us from getting lung cancer if we choose to smoke two packs of cigarettes a day for decades? Wouldn't life be great if we could do what we wanted without suffering any consequences? (Some might call such a place paradise.)

By contrast, the government should be in the business of protecting, defending and upholding the sanctity of life for all. We should be frightened by the idea that the government guarantees women alone will have the power to decide the fate of their unborn child. Men in particular should be afraid and the custody battles that have emerged over the rights to an unborn child are a clarion call.

Consider the atrocities committed by despots and criminals who all believed they had the right to choose life – or death – for another. Will a woman who chooses abortion for her child become less humane as a result of such a decision?

The highest perfection of human life occurs when people are open to God; the ultimate happiness is found in knowing God. When a mother knows God's will, she will try to act as He does – with unconditional love. The late Pope John Paul II argued: "the power for abortion severs the connection with, and the recognition of, the other that defines us as persons."

Teach your children that abortion is contrary to the dignity of the body since the taking of life targets the person. Some make the claim that an embryo is not yet a person. However, geneticists and physicians have made it clear that the genetic code for who a person will become, for all eternity, is present immediately upon fertilization of the egg by the father's sperm. At this stage we are called Zygotes (one-cell life). At this point, a person's eventual height, eye color and most of his or her other physical characteristics are determined.

The developing life goes through stages of development. The first stage is called the *pre-embryonic stage*; it occurs during the first twenty days after conception. The next stage — the *embryonic stage* — occurs from week three through week eight. Most women may have only *guessed* they are pregnant by the eighth week because of missing at least one menstrual period. Women who chart their fertility using Natural family planning methods identify that pregnancy has occurred within twenty-one days after conception. This early knowledge allows mothers to take steps which ensure healthy, early pre-natal care.

By six weeks, brain waves are detectable, and by eight weeks, a baby's heartbeat can be heard. At eight weeks, a developing baby can respond to touch, alternates between periods of sleep and wakefulness, and is active in his amniotic bed. The last stage, between eight and thirty-nine weeks, is known as the *fetal stage. Fetus* is Latin for little one. By ten- to eleven-weeks, a baby's body is completely developed and just needs time, nutrition and protection to develop.

The body expresses the human person. Even while evidencing the need for additional developmental states to achieve viability the developing baby expresses his personhood; true he's very immature but nevertheless he's a person no matter how small. He is not plant nor animal.

All of us have developmental states or milestones to reach. For instance a toddler has yet to develop into an adolescent, an adolescent has yet to develop into a teen, teens have yet to develop into adulthood, young adults have yet to reach senior development, and so forth. Humans keep developing along a continuum from conception onward; this process is halted only by death. Preborn persons are persons from the moment of conception and no one can take their lives without wounding their personal dignity and, in essence, the dignity of all persons.

Abortion procedures: chemical or surgical

There are different abortion procedures available to women and their use largely depends upon the stage of the developing fetus. During the first trimester, women are given the option of a chemical termination or a surgical termination. Whether the abortion is chemical or surgical, the result is the same – a child dies. For your own base of knowledge, I've included a brief description of the different methods commonly used to end the lives of millions of children.

Chemical abortions, sometimes called "medical" terminations, employ the use of steroids and are generally available up through nine weeks gestation. Methotrexate can be used up to seven weeks gestation while Mifepristone, also known as RU 486, can be used up to the first nine weeks of pregnancy.

Emergency contraception, also called the "morning after pill" is a regimen of ordinary birth control pills used in combination and at much higher dosage. Emergency contraception is taken within seventy-two hours of intercourse and a second dosage is consumed twelve hours later. Emergency contraception alters a woman's chemistry in the same manner as birth control pills, preventing implantation of a fertilized ovum. IUDs implanted within five days after intercourse also are used as emergency contraception.

Salt poisoning or saline abortions, a technique developed in the concentration camps of Nazi Germany, were widely used in the first decade after Roe vs. Wade to end first trimester abortions. In this procedure, a salt solution is injected into the amniotic sac as poison for the baby to swallow. Convulsions, hemorrhaging, edema and death occur in about an hour; the mother delivers her dead baby the following day. A similar procedure, called Induction Abortion, is still employed for late term abortions. (See more below).

Prostaglandin drugs were also commonly used to induce violent premature labor and delivery. There is a large complication risk (42.6 percent) associated with its use. It has reportedly fallen out of favor. Prostaglandin drugs were used, however, in the abortion of baby Deborah mentioned earlier in this chapter.

The Kaiser Family Foundation reports that 99 percent of abortions performed in the United States are surgical. Here is a brief description of the various techniques being used. A word of caution: what you'll read here is quite unpleasant.

Suction Aspiration is the surgical procedure commonly employed at six to twelve weeks gestation. During this procedure, a physician will force open the uterus and insert a hollow plastic tube that is connected to a "vacuum." The suction created by this machine, which is twenty-nine times more powerful than a household vacuum, literally tears the newly-developed fetus into pieces, pulling it from the uterus. The physician follows up by cutting the placenta from the uterine wall.

Dilation and Curettage (D&C) begins similarly to Suction Aspiration, except that the uterine vacuuming is followed by the insertion of a curette, a looped steel knife which cuts the fetus and placenta into pieces; the curette is then used as a scraping tool to finish "cleaning" the uterus.

Bleeding is usually more profuse with a D&C. This procedure is often used after a woman suffers a miscarriage, an occurrence the medical community refers to as spontaneous abortion – a naturally occurring process not brought on deliberately for the purpose of terminating a pregnancy.

Menstrual Extraction is a very early suction abortion done before a pregnancy test comes back positive.

In addition to Dilation and Curettage, physicians have developed other procedures for later-term abortions:

Dilation and Evacuation (D&E) is a procedure used when the pregnancy is between fifteen and twenty-one weeks, the stage of pregnancy when the baby's bones have calcified. In the absence of anesthetics for the baby, the physician inserts a pliers-like tool into the uterus in order to seize a leg or other body part. It is then twisted in order to tear it from the baby's body. This procedure is repeated until all body parts are removed. (It's worth noting that the baby's spine must be snapped and his or her skull crushed in order to get it out of the uterus.) The baby's body parts are then pieced together in a pan so the physician can be assured that all parts were removed.

What happens to the baby's body parts after an abortion? They can be ground up in industrial garbage disposals located in abortion facilities, burned in incinerators or thrown into garbage dumpsters, further exacerbating the assault on human dignity. Dead animals oftentimes receive better care than these tiny humans.

Since the development of fertility drugs and the resulting surge in multiple fetuses, intercardiac methods of abortion have grown more common. This procedure is commonly referred to as "pregnancy reduction." Approximately four months into the pregnancy, a needle is inserted through the mother's abdomen, into the chest and heart of one of the multiple fetuses and a poison is injected which kills him or her. When used "successfully," this abortion method results in the dead baby's body being absorbed by the woman's body and the remaining baby developing normally. Oftentimes, though, this method results in the loss of all developing babies.

During the last trimester of a pregnancy, there are two types of surgical abortions available: Induction Abortion and Dilation and Extraction or

Partial-Birth Abortion. It's important to note that fetuses are "viable" from 27 to 39 weeks; this means that upon birth, this fetus (called "baby" by the medical community only after birth) would ordinarily survive.

Induction Abortions involve poisoning the fetus by injecting salt water, urea or potassium chloride into the amniotic sac. This stops the pregnancy by killing the baby and starts the process of uterine contractions so as to speed up the process of delivery. Prostaglandins are inserted into the vagina and Pitocin inserted into the mother's veins to augment the contraction process.

Dilation and Extraction (D&X) or Partial Birth Abortion is also referred to as Brain Suction. It is used after twenty-one weeks gestation. In D&X, a baby that is otherwise viable outside the womb begins a live delivery, but is then killed when the physician inserts a tool into the base of his or her skull in order to suck out the brains.

The dead infant is then fully delivered from his or her mother's womb.

The dangers of this procedure to the mother include amniotic fluid embolism and placental abruption which can cause massive bleeding. Other side effects of this procedure are future cervical incompetence because of the use of forceful dilation of the cervix and uterine rupture weakened after a forced rotation of the fetus during abortion procedures.

Psychological effects after abortions are real for mothers. Some experience some or all of the following: grief, regret, shame, guilt and feelings of worthlessness. Many post-abortive women suffer from insomnia, nightmares, depression, and fatigue. Suicide rates in women who've had abortions are twice as high compared to post-partum mothers.

The future: what can a parent do?

While the vocal on both sides of the abortion issue continue to debate, most Americans remain uncomfortable talking or even thinking about abortion. But parents must be armed with facts in order to teach their children to think critically, act properly, and raise them up the way God meant. Abortion is a scourge on our society and even if it doesn't ever touch your family – it's likely to come close. Remember, one out of every five pregnancies ends in abortion.

It's a sad reality today that many young girls today find themselves pregnant. Many end up feeling alone because of the reaction from those closest to them. Their friends and family voice unconditional opposition to the continuation of a pregnancy. For those girls, abortion becomes a quick way to end these fears of isolation and sense of abandonment. After all, what "choice" did she really have? If you know such a girl, I urge you to show her God's love and compassion, help her emotionally and financially as needed so that she might choose life for her child.

If you have recently discovered that someone has had an abortion, seek help from post-abortion counselors so you learn how best to help her — sometimes we inadvertently lose an opportunity to help others by failing to recognize their distress signals, not knowing what to say or by trying too hard. Learn from the experienced counselors how to reach out and help her find healing.

Christians should remain deeply convicted to ending abortions by working to support women through unplanned pregnancies. These efforts can include any of the following: Helping in your church sponsored pro-life efforts, volunteering at local crisis pregnancy centers or with diocesan-sponsored Project Rachel, support pro-life causes with financial assistance, lobby your legislators, vote pro-life, write to local and national news media, and promote NFP.

As parents, of course, you also have a choice – to love your children and become the teachers who'll help them navigate a society that promotes "anything goes." If you teach your children about the hazards of casual sex (which is why some get into the trouble they do) you can help them see that the sexual freedom touted by society is a lie; true freedom comes only through living God's will.

Casual sex has the potential to hurt us, to make us all feel used, manipulated or even stupid. Anything that promotes casual sex is dangerous to our entire society. Remember, we don't just give our bodies to another person during sex; our entire spiritual, emotional, and psychological being is bound up in our bodies and we cannot afford to be nonchalant about sharing ourselves in such a way. The body is more than a shell; it is where our souls reside. Our body is the Temple of the Holy Spirit, and as such, we deserve to be respected. ❦

chapter seven

Marriage

Remember the children's rhyme: "Johnny and Judy sitting in the tree/ k-i-s-s-i-n-g/first comes love/then comes marriage/then comes baby in the baby carriage." Love. Marriage. Children. This is the path most will walk into vocation.

The term vocation is often misunderstood. Some use the word to describe their job, i.e., a doctor might say his vocation is medicine or a skilled carpenter might call woodworking his vocation. But the words *vocation* and *career* should not be interchangeable. The term vocation is defined as a summons or *calling* to a particular course of action; it's a definition that hints there's a higher purpose reached with vocation than one might attain in mere occupation.

Oftentimes, vocation is the term applied to those entering into a religious order such as to become a priest or a sister. These vocations will be discussed in Chapter eight. While religious vocations are a calling for many, the vast majority of adults will choose marriage as their life's vocation. Because one fruit of marriage is children, the extension of the marriage vocation for women is motherhood and the extension of the marriage vocation for men is fatherhood.

Parents become their children's earliest instructors and models for how to live the vocation of marriage and sadly, these lessons are increasingly moving children and society away from traditional, God-centered values.

Consider these statistics published by the Pew Research Center in 2007:

Roughly one third of all adults have, at one time in their lives, been in a cohabitating relationship. Half of all adults age eighteen and older living in the United States is married compared to 1970, when more than six-in-ten adults were married. Additionally in 2007, nearly four-in-ten births are to unwed mothers compared to one-birth-in-ten to an unwed mother in 1970. Finally, only seven-in-ten children live in two-parent households.

The decline in the number of traditional households and the marked increase in out-of-wedlock births have real implications for our society and are a growing concern for many, mostly older, more religious, more conservative individuals. Younger, more secular adults attach far less moral stigma to out-of-wedlock births, cohabitating without marriage or even divorce as an acceptable resolution to an unhappy marriage. In fact, for some, pregnancy outside of marriage is trendy.

What these statistics mean to you parents is you have your work cut out for you as you proceed to teach your children the importance of not having sex before (or outside) of marriage, the importance of choosing well, the value of committing permanently to a marital relationship, and the importance of rejecting the growing belief that ending a marriage is preferable to staying in a less-than-satisfying one.

Authentic love

Marital love reflects and imitates God's love for us. Father Richard Hogan, expert on Pope John Paul II's *Theology of the Body*, synthesized the following definition of authentic love: "Authentic love must model the same five characteristics of divine love: it must be freely chosen, with knowledge, self-less, permanent, and life giving. If we omit any of these key components when we proclaim love for another, we become but a charlatan for we practice false love."

To love authentically, we must love freely. In other words, love must come through free choice. God loves us unconditionally and He gives us the free will to determine whether we want to love Him back. Many choose not to. It's this same free will that allows us to select the person to whom we proclaim love and commit to spending our life.

Knowledge is the second requirement for authentic love. In order to love God, we must know him; we gain knowledge of God through prayer (communication involving listening and speaking to Him), worship and study. We must put the same effort into knowing the person to whom we pledge our love so that we know that person thoroughly, including all the idiosyncrasies that, down the road, might become difficult to accept.

In order to fully love another, we must give our entire self to that person. We cannot hold part of ourselves back within marriage just as we cannot hold back when proclaiming to love God. Of course, the ultimate gift of self within marriage includes the gift of our sexuality; this gift is so important, it must be shared only within the safety of a permanent marital relationship. Our sexuality is the unique gift we offer our other half which makes us physically one! Coitus lays bare the totality of our gift. We are not ashamed or afraid of our nakedness, our vulnerability, our actions, or the outcomes of the sexual acts in loving, holy marriages; sexuality demonstrates and reinforces authentic love in marriages. Outside of marriage, coitus serves only to garner fear, disgrace, embarrassment, humiliation, dishonor, vulnerability, anxiety, uncertainty and unintentional outcomes between partners. These negative emotions and consequences clearly show us all that these coital acts do not demonstrate authentic love.

When love is permanent, it becomes free and authentic. The gift of self to another within marriage blossoms in an environment of permanence. Another part of our gift of self is freely giving our fertility, another gift from God which should not be presumed or unappreciated. If we withhold this integral part of who we are, we tarnish our love; it becomes selfish. Our children learn the value and beauty of the permanence of marriage through the example set by their parents.

Finally, love must be life-giving as well as life receiving. God doesn't restrict his love for us and neither can we place restrictions on the authentic love relationship that is marriage. Such limitations include the use of contraceptives, which restricts the life-giving power of marital love. When a married couple loves God and accepts His plan for their relationship, they will prayerfully embrace being open to life; using natural family planning, they can even space pregnancies in a way that meets their individual family's circumstances. (See Chapter nine for more on natural family planning.) Couples who authentically love each other will accomplish several things in life: they will help each other get to heaven and they will help increase in each other the capacity to love and become more humane.

When love includes the five characteristics of divine love, the human union found in marriage reflects God and His relationship with man. The Catechism of the Catholic Church states: "The intimate community of life and love which constitutes the married state has been established by the Creator and endowed by him with its own proper laws. God himself is the author of marriage. Marriage is not a purely human institution despite the many variations it may have undergone through the centuries in different cultures, social structures, and spiritual attitudes. These differences should not cause us to forget its common and permanent characteristics."

Authentic Love is fruitful, permanent, with knowledge, freely chosen, and selfless; it perfects as we travel the road to sainthood with our spouse.

Is marriage perfect?

All marriages experience prosperous times when each partner seems happy and healthy and all is well. Likewise, all marriages experience difficult times, such as when one partner becomes ill or losses a job or suffers depression or acts selfish. Our children need to understand that marriage is for keeps during the good times and throughout the bad times too. Children need to see their parents seeking forgiveness and forgiving the other's faults. Marriage can show children that temporary differences and difficulties are just that – temporary. Struggles pass as parents forgive one another and seek God's help and forgiveness as well. This allows the parents to *perfect* their human imitation of God's authentic love.

I consider my marriage to be a happy one, although I'm sure I could relate many challenging times as well. (Fortunately the good days far outnumber the challenging ones.) Early in my marriage I was convinced that my husband would eventually get tired of me and leave. At night, I would dream about women enticing him away from me. I remember vividly the sadness I would then feel after having these dreams. I acted ridiculously, exhausting my poor husband with all kinds of ludicrous questions. His dependability, steady love and faith finally helped me let go of these fears and come to understand that he loved me — unconditionally and permanently. Today, I worry about young brides who might face similar fears but don't have "Dependable Dave" for their husband.

Why did I suffer such fear? Maybe some of it was rooted in the lessons I learned about marriage from my parents – who struggled greatly in their marriage. Their struggles were rooted in their own experiences with their parents' (my grandparents) marriages. My paternal grandparents divorced and their split was something out of a B movie – there was an adulterous act with a best friend that resulted in a child conceived outside of the marital bond. Meanwhile my mother's home life, while not touched by divorce, was colored by economic strife and war, which resulted in her being raised by a young widow who struggled to support a large family.

Neither of my parents experienced what one might consider a happy childhood yet they found in each other a soul mate. Sadly, they often struggled to communicate so at a very early age, I came to understand how even intact marriages can be broken and broken marriages can survive. Sometimes, my sisters and brothers and I wished our parents would end the strife by ending their marriage. Today, I realize that if my parents had gotten a divorce, the cycle of broken relationships would have just continued into the next generation, and so would the pain. So I'm grateful they did the right thing and stayed married. Today my father is deceased and my mother is suffering from Alzheimer's Disease. Before her memory got really bad, she kept saying Dad was coming for her and she needed to go to him. Love, despite the troubles, was evident to me in her words.

Growing up, we all knew divorce was a bad thing – that it was wrong and even carried a stigma. That's not the case today. Because of attitudinal shifts and the availability of no-fault divorces, couples are de-coupling faster and faster and people are casual, almost accepting of divorce without realizing that the effects of a broken marriage will linger for generations. It appears people would rather rationalize the "benefits" of divorce than face the devastating reality of it.

Several years ago, a young couple I knew began to have marital difficulties. To cope, each began to spread details of their pain to those around them, almost as if they were rallying others to their point of view. When the wife reached me with her disparaging comments about her husband, I asked her to stop. I also asked that she stop talking him down to her family and friends and start talking to him to resolve their issues.

Not surprisingly, she became angry with me. It seemed I was the only person who didn't come around to her point of view. Everyone else she spoke to rallied to her defense and encouraged her toward divorce. I admit that at the time I wondered what I had missed as I analyzed her situation. Was I being overly rigid in my viewpoint?

This couple's marriage ended in divorce, but happily this couple has since reconciled and married each other once again; they now have several beautiful children.

My point in sharing this story is simple – marriage is never perfect because it joins two imperfect individuals into a lifelong bond. But marriage, in order to be successful, demands a commitment to working things out when times get tough. Too many people aren't willing to work hard at preserving a marriage once they discover their spouse doesn't live up to their expectations. They look for the easy way out and society tells us that divorce is that exit. But there's nothing easy about divorce. Ask anyone ever touched by it!

Certainly, our spouses come to us with different life experiences, expectations, perhaps even different core beliefs and our own upbringing plays an important role in the person we eventually become. We develop expectations for the world and for others from all the other relationships we've participated in up to the point of marriage, and even beyond. This is why we need to know – really, really know – who we are marrying. We cannot love what we do not know so if we don't learn about our spouse, we can't authentically love him or her.

Additionally, people need to be committed to marriage's permanence in order to eschew divorce as an acceptable solution to marital strife.

Consider for a moment what our children learn about marriage from watching daytime television. What is the message being portrayed about extra-marital affairs by shows such as *Days of our Lives* or *All My Children*? Are affairs presented so commonly that they've become *no big deal*? How often do television shows portray marriage from the perspective of permanence, commitment and real love? If anything, the media likely dissuades young American women from marriage by teaching them marriage equals a mundane, uninteresting existence or that their husbands won't value them once they have children, age, or gain a few pounds. Meanwhile, for our favorite television characters, extra-marital affairs are just routine maintenance to relationships that were never designed to last anyway. What's worse, the consequences to such casual sexual encounters – surprise pregnancies and STDs – are virtually non-existent.

I recommend parents be on their guard with teenagers and especially college-age children so they aren't pulled into the dangerous fantasies proliferated by television shows such as daytime soap operas or night-time dramas. Even romance novels can be dangerous, for these fantasies read like porn for girls – they turn the bad into good and totally ignore the truth about authentic love – that it requires self discipline, self control and a commitment to permanence.

Motherhood: the fruit of a wife's vocation

In order to appreciate and understand motherhood as a vocation, let's look at the truth about the human person. God created each human person with their own intrinsic values and dignity. We are all unique individuals created in the image and likeness of God. Women, by virtue of their femininity, have the unique ability to offer the world hope by giving birth to new life. (Babies are a reminder that God has not forgotten us.) Accepting the role of motherhood implies being open to this new life, which results when a husband offers the gift of himself to his wife, and she accepts. In conceiving a child and then giving birth, a woman discovers her true self through her sincere gift of self returned to both her spouse and to her new child.

It is God's plan that women uniquely desire, and are able through their bodies, to be the recipient of their husband's maleness. Husbands have the unique ability to give their wives the gift of self which co-creates a new life between them. They both have the unique challenge to nurture and mold this co-created gift of life during all the stages of a child's development.

Gender roles are those roles that allow us to act as uniquely female or uniquely male: giving birth, breastfeeding, donating reproductive matter, and including acting in and through our male or female persons. If we deny our gender, we deny that we are created as male or as female yet made in the image and likeness of God; we deny our true humanity.

Not all women are called to be mothers and wives but they are all called to love. Loving women are interested in others, have a nurturing spirit, are generous with others and provide inspiration to those who know them. Conversely women who haven't nourished their capacity to love become bitter, negative, self-serving, selfish and egocentric.

While both husband and wife share parenting of each new child, motherhood brings unique challenges. Only women have the ability to nurture babies with their own milk and this becomes very important to the role of motherhood. Husbands also take on a nurturing role – that of protector

People may give of themselves when engaged in an occupation, but in no way does that match the selfless giving that we're called to as husbands and wives, fathers and mothers.

– and thus each gender assumes a specific role to nurture the family. Together they share many roles, duties and responsibilities.

Wives are called to be the handmaid of their husbands, to love him, accept his maleness and bring forth their children. Mary, the mother of Jesus, demonstrated and modeled for women the true meaning of being a handmaid. She freely served God's will, not as a slave but as a partner. She shows all of us what it means to participate in the dignity of service and for her obedience she reigns as Queen, eternally.

Pope John Paul II in *Theology of the Body* writes: "A woman's dignity is closely connected with the love which she receives by the very reason of her femininity; it is likewise connected with the love which she gives in return."

God created man and woman in his image and likeness. He created us equal – but different. We are part of Him, just like a slice of apple is as much "apple" as the whole apple from which it was cut.

We live in a world busily trying to "equalize" the genders and erase, other than the obvious, any differences between males and females. Some even argue our maleness or femaleness has nothing to do with who we truly are. But if we accept our femininity and its role in motherhood and being wives, we accept God's plan for our life as significant and integral to being a woman.

This does not mean women should not be able to work in the professional career of her choice, especially those in the past reserved for men. There are no longer gender-only professional roles. But the role of father and mother, husband and wife, *are* strictly filled through gender. It is impossible to be a mother if one is male; it is likewise impossible for a woman to claim paternity. Friends of mine who've lost a spouse readily admit they cannot, in their spouse's absence, be both mother and father equally well. Each role is able to be filled by the person whose unique mind, body, soul and will has been determined by God.

Gender roles are those roles which uniquely allow us to act as male or female and as an integrated (body and soul) person. Women who seek to discard the strength of their female role by emphasizing their roles in other areas – such as the workplace – are misleading themselves. We cannot free ourselves from our biological nature without simultaneously ridding ourselves of the spiritual or sacramental. To accept God's design for us means to freely accept our femininity (or masculinity) as defined by Him.

Fatherhood: the fruit of a husband's vocation

Masculinity is often described using images of muscle, brawn, chest hair or intelligence. These are completely inadequate descriptions because they account for only the external male — not the integrated one. Part of the mystery of our existence comes from the fact that we have trouble understanding ourselves beyond the external; to compensate, we often speak in generalities.

When we look at qualities that go deeper than what lies at the surface, we can easily recognize a good man when we see him. He is virtuous. He is a hero. He is the one who unselfishly helps others. Often, he is portrayed as a soldier – the one who serves. It's also easy to identify his antithesis; this man is selfish, egocentric, abandons his family, or is disinterested in having children.

Self mastery and selflessness are qualities that allow a man to be a good husband and a great father. Adam was God's first male creation and God quickly realized he needed a helpmate and companion. That was when God created woman. From this example, we realize it is not good for a man to be alone. A man needs a woman and thus he's called to the vocation of marriage. Within marriage, man receives his helpmate, the bone of his bones. Man is a gift to woman; likewise woman is a gift to man.

His next calling, along with his wife, is to be fruitful and multiply. Being fruitful has nothing to do with making enormous amounts of money or making a name for himself with the press; these are society's goals. Man is supposed to *subdue* the earth; subduing the earth really means giving up those personal pleasures that come as an expense for his wife and children in order to discipline or restrain the wildness in and around him. He is to join with his wife so they no longer are two individuals but one flesh. He becomes the head of the family, and his wife, its heart. Together with their children they form one body in Christ. They are a domestic church.

Man, like woman, is created for marriage for it is through marriage that he and she complete each other in ways integral to creating a family. When each was single, they were complete individuals created in the image and likeness of God but as a married couple, they are more complete when they are together. Simple math tells us that two is more than one.

A man is called to love in his own masculine way just as a woman is called to love in her feminine way. There is nothing subservient, degrading or negative about it. It's only when we invite sin into our lives that the dignity of our relationships degrade and havoc enters the picture. Whenever a man offends a woman's dignity (her vocation) he acts in opposition to his own as well.

Marriage is the only love relationship in which sexual activity can achieve the full meaning given it by God – authentic love. Any other relationship can boast of love, but if it lacks the ingredients found in authentic love, it's a fraudulent relationship, probably based on lust. A marital union in which its participants are not committed to permanence or are closed to new life is not based on authentic love. It does not reflect God's plan for marriage.

Consider a woman who marries without intent to ever have children. Her marriage, if ever challenged, would be considered by the Catholic Church to be invalid. Equally troubling is a marriage where one spouse pursues surgical sterility; by rendering the union infertile, the entire marriage relationship goes dry. A relationship missing the five key characteristics of love is incomplete love, conditional love. In most cases, it will fail. Compare it to building a house on sand; when a storm rages and water surges in, the house gives way under the pressure.

The natural extension of the male vocation is fatherhood. Because a man is called through his maleness to be like Christ, he has a crucial role to fill within the family. Christ so loved us that he took on our sins, suffered and died for us. A man who commits himself to marriage and fatherhood needs to be willing to love his wife and children to the same degree. When his family lives in unity according to God's plan, they are really living in communion with Him. In this way, they also model the Trinity.

Fertility: God's gift

It's been said that female fertility is another one of God's outward signs of the Church's fertility. What does this mean? A fertile Church abundantly spreads new life through God's good news; it evangelizes freely, it brings hope and increases love.

I'm sure you've heard the reference to Christ being a bridegroom and the Church, His bride. Such is the model God intended for both Church and family.

Think about how far, then, we have strayed from God's plan for the Church when we introduce contraception into our families. Not only do we stifle our own fertility – we stifle the Church's fertility too. We also reinvent the Church when we attempt to equalize the sexes in a way that rejects God's design for men and women and further frustrate the Church from growing, evangelizing – in essence, from being fruitful!

Consider the number of clergy-related scandals! Consider also the number of cohabiting couples or babies born out-of-wedlock. These problems coincide with the introduction and widespread acceptance of contraception in our society.

Today, only about 50 percent of marrying couples view marriage as a sacrament – a *permanent* sign of their love and fidelity to each other. Moreover, considerable numbers of men and women deny their dignity by accepting themselves as homosexuals. Hundreds of thousands more abuse their God-given fertility by using contraceptives. Today, many disregard at least one of the Church's teachings, whether it be on matters of faith and morals, including marriage, family life, contraception, or divorce, because these teachings aren't in sync with the times or aren't "politically correct."

An emphasis on a "spiritualized" view of ourselves where males and females are seen as persons "in abstraction" is taking hold. The Catholic Church is leading the battle against this false spiritual philosophy by emphasizing the language of the body as understood by the *Theology of the Body*.

Females can be thankful for their ability to show Christ to the world, to bring Christ to the world and to bring more people to Christ through their unique feminine gifts. Likewise, men can be proud and thankful for their uniquely-male ability to show and bring Christ to the world. Neither can do this merely through career. They must love and lovingly embrace their vocation role including one as husband and wife according to the greatness of God's plan.

Femininity and masculinity reveal the make-up of a person – his or her body, soul and mind. Women have the unique ability to offer the world hope by loving their spouse, and also by giving birth to new life. Fathers offer the world hope by desiring to share his gift of self so his wife may in turn bring forth new life. It takes courage to be a mother. It takes a whole lot of courage to act as a man and become a father. Men and women everywhere need to be courageous in the face of challengers who seek to strip gender from its importance to our vocations.

We were not made to act against ourselves; Jesus' teachings showed us that our bodies, souls and wills are all important to Him as He moved about the Holy Land curing bodies and healing minds with their consent.

A discussion about fertility and creation with your children must also include mention of the importance of the human body and human sexuality, the combination of spirit and matter, and the relationship marital sex has to marital chastity. It's a mistake to believe that one no longer needs to consider "chastity" after one gets married. Chastity has a place within marriage – an important one – just as it had a place before marriage and will have a place after one spouse passes on. All are called to chastity.

What is marital chastity? Marital chastity integrates sexuality with practicality and spirituality. It allows for the integration of the Church's teachings into couples' behaviors. It integrates one spouse's needs into the other's behavior. It fully integrates life and love in each act of intercourse; couples are very aware that their love begets life and love. Marital chastity integrates positive attitude into their lifelong commitment. Marital chastity helps to build a natural defense, a hedge around the intimate relationship.

True intimacy is not compromised by marital chastity; intimate relationships are constructed when spouses serve one another with fidelity while caring for the needs of the other. Intimate relationships do not merely satisfy physical needs; rather they fill up the emotional, spiritual and psychological reserves of their spouse. Marital chastity is achieved with honor and dignity; it is the opposite of lust. Marital chastity fosters self giving and enriches each spouse with joy and gratitude.

It's easy to theorize about how a husband and wife should be totally selfless and giving in their marital relationship, but how can they really? Just as has been described, this is how they do it. They learn it one step at a time, they work through the difficult times, they recognize "dry" times, and they work at their marriage.

The concept of marital chastity also encompasses avoiding a host of evils that are offensive to the marital relationship. These evils include: lust, masturbation, pornography, prostitution, adultery, rape, sodomy, divorce, polygamy, incest and homosexuality. There are more references to be found on the topic of marital chastity in the Catechism of the Catholic Church and I recommend turning to this document to learn more.

How to succeed at marriage

Oh, if only someone had a recipe for a happy marriage!

Marriage blends two unique individuals, one male and the other, female into one couple. Of course, both are human, which means both are imperfect. There will be times when spouses act irrationally or unpredictably and every marriage will experience stress and conflict; its participants will face many, many challenges.

It is by God's design that we have a body, mind and will; all three combine to mold us into the person we are. We have components – psychological, physiological, spiritual, and emotional – that we can never fully understand. But, if we accept that we are an integrated person (body and soul) it's easier to acknowledge that all our composite parts working together are part of what makes us good – and loveable!

Because of our emotional, spiritual and intellectual capacity, we can surprise the world (and ourselves) through our capacity to love others, to be helpful, to be kind, to be understanding, to be patient, to be generous, to be humble, to be .... The list goes on.

By the same reasoning but with the addition of sin, we can surprise the world (and ourselves) by our ability to offend, to hurt, to bring on suffering, to be vengeful, to be jealous, to be .... The list goes on. What's worse, even we can't always predict how we will react to some force pressuring our life or our family on any given day. Imagine, then, the uncertainty that sometimes faces our spouse as he or she tries to predict our response to a given challenge.

Some friends of mine assembled a wedding quilt for me when I married Dave; it contained a cross-stitched "recipe" for happiness, i.e., a dash of humor, a heaping tablespoon of forgiveness, a cup of love, a measure of laughter, etc. I can't recall the entire recipe but isn't life more complicated than this recipe anyway? Or is it? How does one measure out a full cup of love anyway? Of course, it was the thought that counted and the quilt was very pretty; but, maybe its simple philosophy is truer than first implied.

Without a clear "recipe" or plan to achieve marital bliss, how can we ever hope to achieve it? It's simple. You've simply got to want it! There have been plenty of days in my 30-year marriage when I easily could have sat back feeling sorry for myself because my marriage or my husband were light years away from perfect. (It's possible he felt this way once or twice too!) Most days, though, our marriage is a far greater priority for both of us than is our daily dip in the cesspool of self pity. Because we place such a high priority on the survival of our marriage, this attitude of "wanting it" lifts us to become more satisfied with what we have rather than being pulled down by thoughts of what we don't have. We both embrace this attitude about marriage – it is important! Attitude is everything!

A corollary to embracing a positive attitude about your marriage can be found in believing in its permanence. That marriage is forever should simply be a given – never open to debate. If you embrace the expectation that the relationship will endure anything, the critical day-to-day pressures become easier to manage. Studies have shown that when couples have high levels of dedication early in their marriage, such as during the first year, they handle conflict better and report a higher degree of satisfaction with the marriage. But if dedication wanes through time, so does satisfaction.

Before committing themselves to a marriage, both man and woman need to be in complete agreement that divorce is morally wrong, not merely an inconvenience or one of those things that just "happens." Married couples must reject such philosophies. We also need to align our friendships with those who believe as we do. This is not to say that if you encounter a divorced person you are free to act un-Godly toward him or her. Remember Jesus' example to us: hate the sin but love the sinner.

Research shows that persons with strong, traditional religious beliefs are more likely to believe divorce is wrong; those who believe divorce is wrong are more likely to stay in their marriage.

Tell your children that if their beloved is ambivalent about the evil of divorce, a red flag should appear as they contemplate a married life with him or her. If your children haven't ever contemplated their own position on divorce, I urge you to have a discussion with them to shore up their defenses. Pray for them, also, to gain the resolve to stand up for the permanence of marriage at all times.

Dedication isn't merely a byproduct of happiness, though. It's based on personal choice, values and confidence. In other words, dedication to the marital bond is a matter of will. It's something, as humans, that's within our grasp to control! However, we cannot control another's dedication thus it's important to choose a spouse well.

As we work to integrate our body, mind and soul, we actively make choices that affect our actions through our will. If we act with the intent to order our entire life around the good of our spouse, including being open to life according to God's plan, He will send us grace to effectively help us to act more *perfectly*.

Remember, we are all called to become saints. Ask yourself: Do you want to become a saint? Ask the same question of your children.

Another key component to marital bliss is met when both spouses share equal concern for their current or future children's welfare. Should one spouse become careless in his or her affection, duties or care of the children, conflict will no doubt result.

Spouses who do not hold common beliefs about children, their purpose in the marriage, and the belief that transmission of life is a key part of the marriage covenant with God, may soon discover a serious stress fracture in their marriage. Additionally, if one spouse entered the marriage with the intention of never having children, the marriage is an invalid covenant within the Catholic Church.

We should hope and pray for spouses for our children who will share our adult children's values systems and beliefs including the importance of children and the permanence of marriage. Hopefully, we have all instilled in them the truth and expectation that children contribute to the welfare of the couple, the marriage and society in general.

Because of our background as teachers of natural family planning, our children know that couples can learn self control and practice self discipline and marital chastity. Virtuous application of the knowledge of their fertility learned in natural family planning classes keeps couples open to each other and to God's plan for their lives. Couples "form" a family that, with hindsight, reveals God's mysterious hand — it became the right size with the right spacing and the right mix of kids all at the right time.

Having a desire and concern for a spouse's health and wellbeing is another must for a successful marriage. Soon after Dave and I became engaged, Dave made a very simple request of me. He asked that I never say something about him to someone else that I wasn't able or willing to say to him directly. At first, I thought his request to be odd and a bit rigid. Then I considered the consequences of not being able to comply. I thought about what he was asking. If I had a problem with him, why would I want to take that problem to someone else yet be unwilling to address it directly to him? His request made perfect sense and I've tried very hard to honor it throughout our marriage. In fact, it pains me now when I hear a person complain about his or her spouse; I usually wonder why they aren't taking their complaints directly to the source! Negative comments to others about one's spouse serve little purpose other than slandering his or her good name and harming the relationship. This is not the way God wants us to love each other. God loves us despite all of our faults; we are called to model His love.

Inattention to a spouse also can be detrimental to a relationship. Sometimes when I get really busy, my husband can appear too needy or even a burden. Before we married, of course, he was my knight in shining armor.

So what happened? He's the same guy! The problem was, I'd gotten busy, lost focus on my true priorities, and forgotten my vocation. It can be very easy for me to become fixated on meeting an outside goal that I forget my responsibility to my family.

Communicating with a spouse is mandatory to achieving marital satisfaction – and intimacy. Because of gender differences, some couples need to turn to others for help in learning to communicate in the language of love. Wives sometimes hesitate to bring important issues to the forefront for fear that their husband won't hear them. Sometimes one partner withdraws from conflict rather than talking issues through. Problem solving as a couple is more effective when both partners work as a team rather than against each other. All couples will have problems. Some couples combine mutual respect and communication skills to produce a powerful sense that they are a team who works together to find solutions to enhance their marriage. Again, because we have a mind and a will, we have choices in how we deal with problems.

Part of problem solving is bringing to the table a willingness to forgive. It takes a humble soul to set aside pride in the midst of an argument to either admit error or to forgive when a spouse admits a wrongdoing. Forgiveness, then, is paramount to a successful marriage.

Prayer gives us the ability to see our own erroneous ways and gives us a clear insight to the intentions of our spouse. Regardless of how conflict begins, through prayer, we can begin to see what lies behind the heat of an argument and be better able to sort through the problem. When we pray about our conflict, we'll naturally back off from making accusations against our spouse, concentrate on listening to their side of the situation, and more easily find a way to say "I'm sorry." It's hard to tell God my spouse is flawed without admitting to Him a bit more of my flaws also! He also has a way of revealing our flaws to us lovingly. Another trait that we are called to imitate: "Forgive as you have been forgiven… ."

A lack of humility connotes an abundance of pride – something C.S. Lewis calls "the great sin." A truly humble person makes for the best kind of spouse whereas a prideful, arrogant person makes a terrible spouse. Young adults contemplating marriage should be asked: What kind of spouse do you wish to become?

Forces that can impact a marriage negatively come from the prevailing culture. Rather than being influenced by the world, couples committed to love and building a successful marriage need to seek out spiritual influences rather than cultural ones. Positive spiritual influences include regularly attending mass, participating in a parish life, building a prayer life as a couple and as an individual, and seeking out continuing adult education on the faith. Cultural influences to avoid include immoral activities or materials such as porn, most television and movies, adult books, and friends who ridicule God or the Church.

You've heard the phrase: we are what we eat. Well, we also are what we read, see and hear. Things affecting our senses have a powerful effect on us and on our expectations for our life, including our spouse.

Couples need to share common core beliefs and principles. Couples who socialize with other similarly minded couples report they'd be less likely to divorce and more likely to seek out support from others to help them through their trouble.

When Dave and I had just begun to date, I asked him what he thought about abortion. His response astounded me. He said: "Honestly, I haven't given it much thought." How could that be, I wondered. Everyone else around us seemed to have made up their minds and I was so convicted that abortion was immoral that I couldn't fathom not *giving it much thought!* I told Dave that I could never marry a man who thought abortion was OK.

Advise your young adults they should cling to their moral principles as they seek out their life's partner. Dave and I have taught natural family planning classes for years and every now and then I encounter a couple where one spouse has significantly compromised their own moral principles for the sake of the relationship. I met one young woman who years earlier had thought she'd been called to a religious order but who eventually fell in love with an atheist. I prayed the differences in their moral barometers didn't lead them to divorce. It did.

Finding someone who matches your faith becomes a higher priority when you are firmly grounded in that faith. People who grow up receiving more religious education are more likely to marry within their faith. Marrying outside one's faith is commonplace today but it presents many challenges, especially after children enter the picture. The decision on which faith tradition will take precedent in a household is best decided upon before two people enter a marriage covenant. How each person handles these differences will reveal a lot about how they will resolve conflict in other areas of the marriage.

Dave and I were of different faiths at the outset of our marriage. Dave respected the Catholic rule that we raise our children Catholic so our first hurdle was easily overcome. Next, we attended each other's church services every Sunday in order that each of us could fulfill our Sunday obligations. We then attended adult religious education in each other's tradition because neither of us could adequately explain our faith to the other. (What a great learning experience!) Ultimately, one day my husband decided to become Catholic. He wasn't doing it for me; it was a decision between him and God.

Couples should have a positive and supportive social system in place as they begin their marriage. My husband and I have volunteered for the Couple to Couple League for twenty-nine years. During this time, we have taught more than 1,000 couples the art of NFP. We made a host of friends along the way, both teachers and students, all who share our core beliefs. Through volunteering, our friends have become like family and have supported us through the years as we've tried to live out an authentically Catholic marriage.

Spiritual beliefs bring together similarly minded people. From there, couples can develop a social support system to help them succeed in marriage. Clearly, there are benefits to being part of a social group. Studies have shown that members who fit well into their religious community have higher levels of mental health than those who don't. Studies also have consistently shown that people who are isolated are at a greater risk for depression and other health problems, or are susceptible to poverty and suicide. You are much more vulnerable to the stress of life when you have no social support system.

Religious involvement brings with it ready-made social structures. Religions specify codes of behavior and rituals that naturally connect those involved. Social links to a community are important for couples. When a couple shares a core belief system, they share a common "view of the universe." A shared view of the world includes having a mutual understanding about the meaning of life, death and marriage, which supports the idea of lifelong commitment. It should generate mutual respect.

Before marriage, couples need to make an investment in each other. That means they should spend as much time together as possible, shield each other from dangers to their self esteem and dignity, and get to know each other's strengths and weaknesses. They need to learn how to build a "hedge" around themselves which shields the relationship from intrusive forces, such as developing a crush on another person. This hedge must remain in effect throughout their marriage.

Research has shown that individuals who have affairs do so not because their marriage was unhappy but because they became emotionally or physically attracted to another person. The concept of building hedges is wonderfully outlined in the book *Loving Your Marriage* by Jerry Jenkins. Young people contemplating marriage need to know that even after ten, fifteen, or twenty years of marriage, spouses can still develop a crush on another person. When that happens and they first become aware that another person impacts them in that "special" way, it's important that they act quickly to protect themselves against acting foolishly. I recommend anyone entering a marital commitment read Jenkin's book.

Preparing for marriage

Young adults contemplating marriage need to attend worthwhile marriage preparation programs and natural family planning classes. (The Couple to Couple League is one of several NFP providers; it offers instruction in the Sympto-Thermal method of NFP.)

Also couples should begin to build their hedges and draw closer to their religious roots. They should talk, talk and then talk some more so their expectations and dreams begin to merge into one. By the time a man and woman get to the point of saying their vows before God, they should share a world view and a core belief system and respect their differences.

In conclusion, marriage does not promise an easy life but rather a happy life. A purposeful life. A joyful life. Marriage in Christ promises love will conquer all difficulties, even death. Married love is, to quote the famous vow: for better, for worse, for richer, for poorer, in sickness and in health until death do us part. Married love should bring each of us to Heaven's door.

The marriage vocation can be difficult to be sure. But remember, God spared his own Son so that we may be certain that He will not refuse us anything. Faithfulness in marriage reveals Jesus's gospel promise that the fullness of joy will go to those who remain in His love and keep His commandments.

People may give of themselves when engaged in an occupation, but in no way does that match the selfless giving that we're called to as husbands and wives, fathers and mothers. If one professes to love God, one must actively seek a relationship with God, meaning they must seek knowledge of Him and remain in communion with His will. The marriage vocation allows husband and wife to give of each other in a unique way as together they raise children and seek out communion with God.

You've no doubt heard the phrase "it takes a village to raise a child." I prefer this quote from former U.S. Ambassador to Gambia, George Haley: "It takes a strong family to create a village."

It's the family that teaches the village about God, the importance of marriage and children. Parents who assume their proper responsibilities as fathers and mothers have no need to bring childrearing into the public square. Certainly they may seek assistance from "villagers" for guidance when the village supports their belief systems, but remember that no village on earth can teach a child about love and marriage better than a mother and father who love and accept God's will for their marriage. ❦

chapter eight

Religious Vocations

I would be remiss when writing this book if I omitted mention of religious vocations. Why? Because this book is for real families with real children and from these families come our priests, sisters, brothers and deacons.

Many, many men and women eschew the marriage vocation in order to permanently devote themselves to God by entering a religious vocation. Many options are open to those who seek a "religious" life: priest, brother, monk, sister, or nun. (A religious vocation open to a married man is permanent deacon.) Additionally, a religious vocation can be contemplative, semi-contemplative or active.

All who take vows to live a religious life accept celibacy and obedience to God as the constitution by which they'll order their lives. Additionally, many religious also take a vow of poverty, giving themselves over to a life of self sacrifice and physical denial. Chastity is just as integral a part of living a religious vocation as any other life in service to God.

Religious men and women take vows for the purpose of making a promise to God as special witnesses. They vow to live simply and renounce the basic ways of the world that lay people typically cannot because they're charged with raising families.

Not everyone is 100 percent clear on the difference between a monk, a brother, and a priest – or the difference between a sister and a nun. Nearly everyone at one point in their life, though, is curious about the lives lead by the "religious." In order to help you explain this path to your children, I've included some information culled from several resources. Because my experience and training lies solely in the Roman Catholic tradition, I'll restrict my explanation of religious vocations to only Catholic religious orders.

Orders are the term commonly used to describe religious vocations. Orders are vows taken to live under stricter religious standards than are required of the laity (members) of a specific faith tradition.

Types of religious vocations

Religious vocational opportunities are different for men and women; they also can be defined as contemplative, semi-contemplative or active.

Contemplative orders focus primarily on prayer in a monastery setting that sets members apart from society. Within contemplative orders, women are known as nuns and men are known as monks. Nuns and monks follow rigid schedules involving solemn prayer, personal prayer, physical denials and self-sacrifice. Most members also participate in some sort of physical labor whether it is upkeep of the community, the production of food, or producing goods for sale to earn income for the community. Papal enclosure rules are in force to keep a separation between contemplative orders and the rest of society.

Semi-contemplative orders resemble contemplative orders in many ways, but they also supplement prayer through good works in the community. Semi-contemplative orders characterized much monastery and convent life beginning in the seventeenth century all the way to the late twentieth century.

Active orders set aside traditional monastic life to respond to the needs of the sick and the poor, first in Europe and later in the west. With active orders, the physical structures that abetted the isolated monastic life of solemn prayer were relaxed. Instead, the focus became providing educational, medical and outreach services to the young, poor, sick, and needy. Men in active orders are called brothers or priestly clerics while women in active orders are called sisters.

Some sisters and brothers wear religious habits as an outward sign of their consecration to God. Others do not, preferring instead to be viewed as one with the people they serve rather than standing apart from them. The church treasures the variety of ministries and expressions of religious life for its "charisms" and thus approves both those who wear habits and those who do not.

A monastery is what you call the home for contemplative and semi-contemplative religious orders. A convent, meanwhile, is the name for a home for a community of active-order sisters. The woman who is elected to lead the nuns of a specific monastery is called an Abbess and her monastery is called an Abbey. An Abbess's male counterpart is called an Abbot. Abbots and Abbesses rank in authority equal to diocesan bishops, yet Abbots and Abbesses still require the services of a priest in order to celebrate Mass or perform other sacramental duties.

During the nineteenth century, when immigration to America peaked, more than six hundred active religious orders were founded in Europe; their members became the backbone of the movement to build and staff parochial schools, hospitals and other agencies that served America's growing immigrant Catholic population.

There are two types of deacons and two types of priests. A permanent deacon is an ordained minister who can perform many sacramental functions, such as baptisms or marriages, but who cannot say Mass or consecrate the Eucharist. Permanent deacons are typically married men who go through the Diaconate in addition to working in the professional arena. Once these men are ordained as permanent deacons they are no longer able to remarry if their spouse should die, or, if they are single when becoming ordained, they would not be free to marry.

A transitional deacon is different from a permanent deacon; a transitional deacon is a step away from ordination into the priesthood.

Priests come in two varieties as well: diocesan priests and religious order priests. Priests typically do not take a vow of poverty during ordination but they do make a vow of chastity and obedience to the magisterium, the teaching authority of the Catholic Church. Both types of priests are equal in the priesthood faculties they acquire through ordination but they differ in their way of life, the type of work they do, and the church authority to which they answer. Diocesan priests commit their lives to serving the people of a diocese, (a church's administrative region) and generally work in parishes, schools or other institutions, as assigned by their bishop. Religious order priests belong to orders such as the Jesuits, Dominicans, or Franciscans. In addition to vows of obedience and celibacy taken by diocesan priests, religious order priests take a vow of poverty.

The vows taken by religious men and women allow them to live simply, renounce the many ways of the world, and adopt a non-materialistic lifestyle. Additionally, the vow of celibacy or chastity gives religious men and women unity of mind, body and will to God, who becomes their spouse. Finally, the vow of obedience assures us that religious men and women listen to God's voice, as expressed through church leadership, and respond to it as fully as possible.

One additional vow – of stability – is required of some religious orders such as the Benedictines. This vow means a member will remain with a single monastic community for his or her entire life. The vow of stability is comparable to the aspect of permanence in the marriage covenant.

Diocesan priests attend to the spiritual, pastoral, moral and educational needs of the members of a parish community. Their day usually begins with morning meditation and/or Mass. Often, they receive spiritual direction or other counseling on matters of importance to their ministry. They also often perform pastoral duties, such as home and hospital visits to the sick of their community. They can serve and lead church committees, work with civic and charitable organizations, and assist in community projects. They also prepare parishioners for marriage and other sacraments.

Permanent deacons can perform many of the traditional functions of the parish too. Permanent deacons have been ordained to preach and perform liturgical functions such as baptism, marriage, and funerals and to provide service to the community, i.e, to the sick, widows and orphans. Permanent deacons bring *viaticum* to the dying. Deacons cannot celebrate Mass nor administer the sacraments of reconciliation or anointing of the sick, but they do represent a bridge between the laity and the clergy being a member of both communities.

Today's priests are highly educated. Most enter theological seminaries after earning a college degree. There are currently forty-six seminaries in the United States. In order to be ordained to the priesthood, a man must earn either a Master's of Divinity degree or a Master's of Arts degree. Theology coursework includes: sacred scripture; dogmatic, moral, and, pastoral theology; the art of preaching; church history; sacraments, and church law. Priests are encouraged to continue studies at least informally after ordination, particularly in the social sciences such as sociology and psychology.

Religious order priests receive duty assignments from the superior in their respective religious order. Some religious priests specialize in teaching whereas others serve as missionaries in foreign countries. Some religious priests live a communal life in a monastery where they devote their lives to prayer, study and assigned works.

We should all pray for priests who will be counselors and spiritual guides of individuals and families.

Both types of priest can and do hold teaching and administrative posts in Catholic seminaries, colleges and universities, and high schools. Religious priests staff university level positions and many high schools not associated with parishes. Diocesan priests usually are concerned with parochial schools, meaning schools attached to a parish, although they also may serve at diocesan high schools.

Priests are commonly addressed as father; often, spiritual leaders are addressed as "father" because of the spiritual relationship they have to us, the laity. Priests are the shepherd of their flock; they assume a fatherly role as protector and teacher.

Who is called?

One who truly loves God and who calls others to love God will do so one of two ways: through the sacrament of marriage or the sacrament of holy orders. In essence, then, it is all who are called!

When you love someone, you want the best for them and you give the best of yourself in return. This can lead to large demands. We get shaken from a life rooted in mediocrity and get put on our feet toward a lifelong journey to become the best, most perfect, noblest, holiest human imaginable. A saint!

Mother Angelica of EWTN once admitted she'd felt anxiety when as a young girl she read accounts of saints' lives. It bothered her that she hadn't encountered "fat saints, ugly saints, saints with big noses, frowning saints, tired saints." The perfection with which these accounts were colored discouraged her. The biographers made the saints unrealistic by making them perfect, she recounted. "They were always kind, always patient, and always able to resist temptation."

Despite the biographers' omissions, the majority of saints were indeed ordinary people who struggled with temptation, sin, frailties and weakness in the same way we struggle with temptation, sin, frailties and weakness. Of course, God wants us to become saints and He also calls some of us to become religious sisters, brothers, or priests. The path toward heaven weaves through religious vocations just as it weaves through the marriage vocation.

In a materialistic society, those who follow in the footsteps of Christ are often labeled bigots, fanatics or dreamers. Certainly, being on fire for the Gospel makes you a radical – but in the most positive fashion! How else can one live for the cause of Christ and his Church but with passion? And how can true love ever be dispassionate? When you love, you give your whole self to the object of your affection; it is the same when you love Christ and decide to commit yourself to Him. Such a commitment requires one hundred percent of your time, focus and energy.

As we learn by reading the Gospel, Jesus sent his apostles to do work for the people, to heal the sick, raise the dead, cleanse the leper and drive out the demons. In themselves, the apostles were very weak and untalented people: fishermen, tax collectors, zealots. The apostles showed all the weaknesses of ordinary people but Jesus continued to count on them to get the job done simply because He knew the grace and power of the Holy Spirit; the Spirit guided them and protected them and gave them *awesome powers despite their human frailties.*

We hear frequently reasons for the dwindling numbers now attracted to religious vocations: a weakened family life; negative press related to scandals; the magnetic pull of the secular world, or celibacy. These are society's reasons. Certainly, the devil is at work in this realm too.

But Jesus gave us a more positive message: Pray to the Lord of the Harvest to send laborers into our midst. His message is: don't harp about shortages but pray for vocations! What a simple yet positive and powerful command.

So maybe He is calling someone in your family. Do you know with certainty that your son or daughter is not being called to the religious life? Or are you 100 percent certain that if they did feel called that you'd support them?

First and foremost, children need to be taught that the primary question of human existence is: What does God want me do with my life? That's different from asking: What do I want to do with my life?

A deeper question to ponder is: "Why was I born?" Did God have a specific purpose in mind when He created your son or your daughter? If so what might be that purpose?

Recall the prayer of St. Francis: It is in giving that we receive and it is in dying that we're born to eternal life. Dying to self and selfish interests, that is.

Trends

Since 1800, the Catholic Church in the United States has grown from one diocese and thirty-five parishes to 192 dioceses and more than 19,000 parishes. Yet even though the Church is growing, statistics reveal the number of people accepting a religious vocation continues to decline.

Activity for religious orders peaked during the 1800s, when 600 new religious communities were formed. In the last four decades of the twentieth century, 147 new religious communities were organized in the United States.

In 1950, more than 75 percent of all Catholic school teachers were religious sisters; today, 93 percent of Catholic school teachers are lay persons. Participation in religious orders peaked during the 1960s: in 1965 there were 181,421 religious sisters, in 1966, there were 12,539 religious brothers, and in 1967 there were 23,021 religious priests. Diocesan priests aside, there are 103,000 religious in the United States today; approximately 21,000 are men (half of those are older than sixty-one) and 82,000 are women (half of those are older than sixty-eight).

In 2006, there were roughly 47,500 priests in the United States (17,000 religious and 30,500 diocesan) with sixty-three being the average age for religious priests and fifty-nine the average age for diocesan priests. Moreover, fewer than one in five diocesan priests are younger than forty five years old.

Clearly, the world needs people convicted about their faith to become spiritual leaders.

A lay ecclesiastical ministry is new and increasingly important. In 2006, more than 26,000 lay ministers have joined the formal leadership within parishes, dioceses and Catholic organizations. More than 30,000 are enrolled in formation programs for professional ecclesiastical ministers. Additionally, an active permanent deaconate program is helping to compensate for the decrease in new priests. Lay people are being called on in greater numbers to help with their parishes, which for many years was the sole responsibility of the pastor. Shortages, therefore, have opened the door to creative solutions and more of these are likely ahead of us as fewer priests and religious step forward to accept God's call. It is important, therefore, to pray for more religious vocations.

I do not expect (nor would I suggest) that the ordination of women or the dissolution of the celibacy vow would permanently reverse any downward trends in the numbers of new priests and religious.

What about married priests?

Diocesan priests minister to families – husbands, wives, parents, children, brothers and sisters. The role of their ministry is to provide Christ's truth and message to these families and to provide them with the sacraments so that God's grace is extended to all the faithful. Can priests perform this ministry without the first-hand experience of being in a marriage? Yes!

From the moment I got married, I presumed and anticipated that one day soon I would become a parent. The second I conceived my first child, I became a parent (whether I was ready or not!). Even though no one gave me an instruction book guaranteeing my success, I knew I didn't need to parent for ten years before becoming qualified. I could be a great parent right from the start!

Similarly, a priest doesn't have to be in a marriage to teach married couples the truth of Jesus Christ. He doesn't have to be married to bring God's blessed sacraments to families. The qualities of good priests include being a good communicator, a good listener, a moral person, and above all else, a person who loves God above all others. He should be a person who wants to share this gospel message with passion and devotion. He does not need firsthand experience on marriage and child rearing.

While married couples may often have to resort to marriage counselors who themselves are married for practical help within their marriage, one does not need to be married to understand the theological, sacramental, and church laws regarding marriage.

Priests embrace the gift of celibacy in order to more fully devote themselves to the Church. I have talked with many young priests who all see that marrying would place a strain on a family. One priest also asked me to consider the financial burden a priest with six to ten children to raise might place on an already struggling parish.

Why can't women be priests?

Only men are called to the role of ordained priest because of the distinction God Himself made when He created men and women. When Jesus called only men to become apostles, He acted in a completely free and sovereign manner, writes Pope John Paul II in *Theology of the Body.* In other words, Jesus acted without regard for human being's social graces or conformities. Being God, He was not in need of affirmation for any of his actions. Jesus was decidedly countercultural. He talked with a woman at the well, showing us that women had dignity despite cultural mores of the times that might have said otherwise. (Women normally carried a lower status than men.) Here was the son of God, born of a woman, showing us that women are equal in dignity to men, a dignity borne out of being a creature of God.

Just as Jesus didn't follow norms regarding women, he certainly didn't call society's most respected men to become his apostles and to carry forth his word. He chose a tax collector, a betrayer, and mere fishermen.

When Jesus called his apostles to perform the Eucharistic celebration, He conferred sacramental powers on the twelve who in turn passed these powers onto new priests through the laying on of hands. This was how Jesus ordained priests. The priesthood follows "apostolic succession;" this means your local priest can trace his priestly roots all the way back to the apostles and to Christ himself. In the Eucharist, Christ links priestly service to the apostles, all men. He expresses the proper relationship between the mystery of the creation and the mystery of the redemption...as sacramental minister of the Eucharist, the priest acts *in persona Christi*, in the person of Christ.

When churches "ordain" women to the ministry, they are simply not following apostolic succession in principle or practice. Christ didn't pick women to be priests, even though priestesses were common in many pagan religions of His time. God did not select women to serve in the sacramental mission of the church; He gave them other roles which shouldn't be viewed as secondary or less important. Women's roles are just different. Only society and people with high ambitions view the ordination of men to the priesthood as discriminatory and sexist. Similarly, those who equate priesthood with secular power also object to the appearance of "discrimination."

The mystery of the creation involves women; Eve and Mary are the predominant figures here. Recall Mary, Martha, and the other women who followed Christ; none of these women clamored to be a priest or have an equal opportunity at apostleship. Mary certainly would have been the most qualified. But she held a different, more revered, role: mother of Christ.

Women need to embrace their femininity and service to God in the manner that He created, not in the roles that men and women carve out for themselves.

To insist that women need to be ordained or have the opportunity of ordination is to deny God's natural role for men and women. It also denies that God intended them to have another natural role specific to their maleness or femaleness. These roles do not negate the fact that men and women share a specific yet distinct value.

The push for a female priesthood resembles a clamor from some who say: "I don't want to be a woman. I'd rather be a man." It's a myth that the true dignity of women exists only when she can act like, or have the same opportunities as, a man.

The church has always fully attended to women in their various roles. Through the centuries, women have been in large measure the ones responsible for passing along the faith to children. Women have also been holy martyrs, virgins and mothers who bravely bore witness to their faith and passed on the tradition by bringing up their children in the Spirit of God.

One woman is indeed most blessed of all humans; this person is Mary. Jesus loved his mother and she is blessed among all women. As Queen of Heaven, she could be considered to have out-flanked all of the apostles, martyrs and saints. Yet, the Mother of God would merely think of herself as the lowliest of all handmaidens.

When riding the tide of change that is our times, we can only connect the dignity of women to their vocation by returning to our foundations which is found in Christ – to those immutable truths and the values of which he himself remains the faithful witness. Again, God created two different means for both genders by which they can spread his kingdom – marriage and religious vocation. Both types of vocations carry unique roles, and burdens to bear while growing God's Church.

The Church supports and upholds the dignity of all women. The Church has a longstanding tradition of educating its women and passing along its traditions and faith through women. Long before secular institutions believed it practical to educate women, the Church created women's colleges to educate its sisters and laity.

Religious women renounce marriage and motherhood and accept virginity and a distinctive protector role for Christ. The renunciation of motherhood can involve great sacrifices for a woman; it also opens them up to serve in a different kind of motherhood – motherhood according to the Spirit. Sisters are devoted to nurturing and protecting many – the needy, the sick, the homeless, the hungry, the elderly, the terminally ill, special needs children, and even those who are imprisoned.

Pope John Paul II reminds us again: "Spousal love always involves a special readiness to be poured out…." A sister's spouse is the person of Jesus Christ. Together, they work to help others. This is what their spouse asks of them: what so ever you do for the least of my brothers, you do it for me. Fulfilling this request is no less demanding and no less fulfilling than administering the sacramental duties of priestly service.

Clergy abuse

I understand that the Catholic Church is not perfect.

Jesus handpicked twelve men to be his disciples and all but one, John, betrayed or turned away from our Lord at least once. Judas, of course, directly betrayed Jesus, handing Him over to die on the cross. In terms of loyalty among the twelve, which included Judas, the disloyalty rate (one out of twelve) comes out to roughly 8.33 percent.

In 1995, when clergy abuse cases began making front page news, there were 49,000 priests in the United States and 500 of them were accused of wrongdoing.[1] That's a scandal rate of just more than 1 percent. This statistic is questioned by many as being too low; regardless it doesn't begin to approach the 8 percent of the apostolic era. Of course, in terms of victims, any number of abusers is too many.

Sadly, the Catholic Church isn't the only church that has been marred by scandal. The Presbyterian Church stated recently that 10 percent to 23 percent of its clergy has admitted inappropriate sexual behavior or contact with others. Research in 1990 among the United Methodist Church revealed 38.6 percent of its ministers had sexual contact with a church member and 77 percent of church workers had experienced some type of sexual harassment. The United Church of Christ found that 48 percent of woman in the workplace had been sexually harassed by male clergy. The Southern Baptists claim 14.1 percent of their clergy have sexually abused a church member.[2]

I bring these statistics forward to silence those who point to priestly celibacy as the root cause of these abuse cases. Celibacy is not the issue. The problem stems from seminaries ordaining pedophiles, and individuals with serious psychological disorders not discovered or revealed during seminary formation. It's faulty logic to believe that if priests were allowed to marry, these abuse cases would disappear, especially considering the disheartening abuse statistics from other Christian denominations.

The only truth regarding these scandals is that the cost to its victims and their families can not be tallied. Too many lives have been destroyed; too many victims have turned to alcohol, drugs, unsafe sex, violence or suicide. The cost of clergy abuse among its victims may never be tallied.

Clergy abuse has also cost the Church – in disillusioned membership, damaged reputation, and diminished esteem for all the good priests who are doing God's work. Pope Benedict XVI's recent apology to victims of clergy abuse should help the healing process and reunite hurting Catholics within the Church. Catholics need to be aware that good priests are also under attack simply because of their passion for God; we need to be helpful to them when and however we can.

We need to help restore the priestly vocation to the respectful standard it once enjoyed and reinforce in our children who might be hearing a call to the priesthood or religious life that God needs them more than ever to help grow His Church in a special way. Furthermore, we need to uncover all Church scandals in order to help the Church help Her people. We have to also trust that God continues to bless while disciplining His growing Church.

Clergy abuse scandals have allowed the Church to begin cleaning its house. One doesn't clean a house when you don't see the dirt! The priests who commit offenses against others must never be sheltered nor allowed to repeat their offenses. Woe to the priest who leads anyone astray. But the laity must be held to the same standard. Woe to any of us if we lead our children astray! We need to tend to our children's spiritual needs and not allow them to wander away from their faith.

We should all pray for priests who fit the late Pope John Paul II description: "...Counselors and spiritual guides of individuals and families. He should be able to teach about the church's teaching on marriage and sexuality without ambiguity. He should be the first to give a good example of goodness, and have internal loyalty to the church and Christ. He should exhibit external obedience to the teaching authority of the church, and teach truth. He should speak the same language of the magesterium of the church to others, united of same mind, and judgment, and believe that the saving teachings of Christ are what in turn saves souls and is good for souls (the highest form of charity). He should practice patience and be of sole purpose to save while showing mercy to individuals. He should be an echo of the Redeemer's voice and love. Ideally he should strive to be a confident speaker, fully convinced that the Spirit of God assists the magesterium with proposing doctrine. He should ask the Spirit of God to light the hearts of the faithful so they can listen and learn. He is to teach prayer by being himself prayerful and hopeful and not easily discouraged by his own weakness or the weakness of those around them."

These are big shoes and ones not easily filled on our own accord. But the same can be said for marriage. If it wasn't for the Divine grace received from these sacraments, I doubt many of us would define our current state in life as successful.

When one explores the possibility of entering an order for religious life, it's a good idea to compare several different orders first by observing the members, seeing how they function and volunteering to gain an insider perspective. Even Internet research can be helpful if one is initially curious about the lives and works of a certain religious order.

It is also a good idea to contact your diocesan director for religious vocations, a recent religion instructor, or a pastor, to help navigate the myriad possibilities and options for religious life. Some universities offer a Catholic studies group which may be further helpful to discern whether a religious order is part of God's plan for the future of someone you love. ❦

chapter nine

Fertility

We are a country that by and large equates contraceptive use with responsible behavior. This attitude almost always puts couples who decide to bear a multitude of children or those who believe contraception jeopardizes marriages in the position of having to defend their "recklessness." As a result of increased pressure to conform our behavior to societal expectations, the birthrate in the U.S. and other developed nations has dropped throughout the twentieth century.

My husband, Dave, and I have seven children; we are just one of many couples who dismiss society's call to use contraceptives as responsible and good for marriages. (Statistics show us otherwise.) Instead we chose to build our family using natural family planning with the hope of discovering God's plan for our family's ultimate size. We are happily raising our large family despite encountering hostility from people antagonistic toward large families. Some even point to the number of children we have as *proof* natural family planning doesn't work.

I have had people say to me:

"Nobody *wants* seven children."

"Your husband must be quite a stud!"

"Were you drunk?"

"I feel sorry for you!"

People have also made the following inappropriate comments to my children:

"Your mother has too many kids."

"Don't your parents believe in birth control?"

Clearly, a society that views intolerance as one of its great sins is still willing to embrace intolerance when it comes to judging large families.

Dave and I built our large family intentionally; in truth, we are very blessed to have seven children. Along the way, we had one miscarriage and that loss helped remind us that fertility is truly a gift from God. It is to be cherished and treasured, never assumed or mistreated. Similarly, we must always be on guard against making assumptions about small families. A family with only a few children might mean the parents have suffered repeat miscarriages or fertility problems. Or, they could face serious issues that require them to limit the size of their family. Not every couple is physically capable of producing a large family and not every couple invites contraception into their relationship.

For all who ponder whether to use contraception versus natural family planning, Pope John Paul II provides clarity: "Couples practicing NFP tend to have more children than couples who contracept, not because the method is less reliable but because these couples come to appreciate the importance of children to their marriage and they want to become generous with God."

Natural family planning techniques are effective! Often, though, couples who adopt NFP discover they become more open to the idea of children (as cited earlier by Pope John Paul II) because they view fertility as a symbol of hope, of springtime – a time of renewal. Contrast this to the changes brought about in a woman using contraceptives; she suffers from a self-imposed, artificially prolonged infertility, much like a pond frozen in perpetual winter. This negatively affects her libido as well. (Her spouse suffers likewise.) This chilly outlook on new life spreads throughout society. Bleak outlooks increase pessimism and fuel hedonism and individualism. Look around and see for yourself the negative traits and habits that have become common to many marriages. Many married people can't or won't defend the specialness of their marriage when confronted by same-sex marriage advocates. This leads many to lack regard for the sanctity and extraordinariness of marriage between men and women.

How did this lack of regard for marriages begin? Perhaps, wide-spread contraception use in and out of marriages have helped fuel this profound disregard. Let's analyze this.

Contraception: an insipid influence

You will not find references to contraception in the Bible just as you won't find guidance on the use of the Internet in the articles of the Constitution that address freedom of speech. We live in a different time from when these two important documents were drafted. That is why we look to the Church to guide us on morals just as we look to the government to guide us on matters of law. The Bible does, however, offer us this instruction on life: be fruitful and multiply.

The Catholic Church draws its teaching authority from two sources: the Bible (Gospels and more) and magisterial teachings, which flow through the Holy Spirit to the Pope and are subsequently passed by way of apostolic succession all the way to you through your parish priest. The Church teaches: We are made in God's image and likeness. If we accept this, we also accept that we have been given free will to love God, trust Him and follow His commandments. Or, we can reject God. Whatever our choice becomes, though, God continues to love us. Wow!

Have you ever wondered if God looks at us humans and wonders: Why did I ever make these clowns? We need to understand that God clearly and emphatically remains overjoyed by all of His creations, especially we human beings. Consider the good things humanity has accomplished because of God's many graces through the centuries. Consider the fact that He even allowed his Son to grace earth with His presence, to heal us, to teach us, to die for us, to forgive us. If God wished He'd never made humans or the world, He would actually be acting against His very nature! So it is impossible for God to regret our creation. He loves us unconditionally, permanently, and with full knowledge. What's more, He is continually life-giving and love-giving.

In the middle of the nineteenth century, with America populated by a Protestant majority, most every Christian denomination agreed that contraception was evil and therefore its use and distribution in the United States was outlawed. But Protestant churches slowly veered from this thinking by the close of the twentieth century leaving the Catholic Church to stand alone among Christian churches in its opposition to contraception. This shift was first detected in 1930, when an Anglican bishop assembled for the Lambeth Conference wrote on the topic: "Where there is clearly-felt moral obligation to limit or avoid parenthood, the method must be decided upon Christian principles ... primary and obvious method is complete abstinence from intercourse. Where there is a morally sound reason for avoiding complete abstinence, the conference agrees that other methods may be used... ."

It was a small crack, but the door to widely-accepted contraceptive use was indeed opened as Anglican Church authorities gave credence to an emphasis on personal conscience when it came to deciding how to respond to the moral question: should we become parents?

By the 1958 Lambeth Conference, the Anglican Church went a step further, saying the responsibility for deciding upon the number and frequency of children has been laid by God upon the consciences of parents everywhere; that this planning ... is right and important factor in Christian family life. Three years later, the National Council of Churches stated: "most of the Protestant churches hold contraception and periodic abstinence to be morally right when the motives are right." As long as the motives were moral, the methods didn't matter.

Fast forward to today. Some churches in their literature for engaged couples actually promote contraception as "safe and simple" — and responsible.

In 1930 when the Anglican Church took its stand on the issue of contraception, the issue was clearly a topic for married Christians to ponder. Not so today. Think about the messages targeted to teens by those who want to provide open access to contraception in public schools. "We know that abstinence is probably the best," the message goes. "But most of you won't and can't practice it so we are here to offer you birth control (or abortion)." What are these well-meaning but misguided folks really saying? "Kids, as long as you consent to what you are doing, make sure it's safe sex. Stop by the school-based clinic today!"

Furthermore, vaccinating young pre-teen girls against STDs, and prescribing birth control pills to wash away acne or reduce menstrual cramps, sends the same pessimistic message. There are other ways to deal with these matters than using veiled messages which are negative, destructive and contrary to training children into chastity.

As I stated earlier, I have seven children. Also, I came from a family of seven children. This might lead you to believe my parents have many,

We are not replacing ourselves in adequate numbers and the consequences to society are significant.

many grandchildren. Actually, they only have thirteen grandchildren and eleven great-grandchildren — my children account for more than half of the grandchildren. Recently a couple from our parish celebrated their sixtieth wedding anniversary. They had ten children but only eighteen grandchildren and even fewer great-grandchildren. The newest generations of this family are not replacing the older generations – a situation growing more commonplace and also evidenced by my own family.

We, as a society, are not replacing ourselves in adequate numbers and the consequences are significant. Soon, as Baby Boomers enter retirement, America will face a severe shortage of workers. What's more, Social Security will have fewer workers supporting greater numbers of retirees. Also, the demands for housing will shift, educational pressures will increase, medical costs will continue to rise, and the tax burden will be carried by fewer workers.

Look at your own family in terms of replacement numbers a few generations down the road. Where does it stand? Today's family generally produces 2.2 children – roughly a neutral effect in terms of individual replacement. (Extrapolating this forward, a family with two children would have four or five grandchildren and eight or nine great-grandchildren. By contrast, a family with a more positive replacement might be a couple with five children, twenty grandchildren and forty great-grandchildren.)

When the Anglican Church took its initial pro-contraception stance in 1930, several bishops warned that they would be "opening up a Pandora's box to many ills if they accepted contraceptive use." In 1936, U.S. federal courts permitted doctors to import contraceptive devices on the grounds that Congress had intended an earlier ban to apply only to the immoral use of contraceptives, not the moral use, such as when contraceptives might be prescribed by a doctor. Suddenly, physicians replaced priests, rabbis and ministers in helping couples to decide whether their delaying or avoiding pregnancy would be considered moral. That same year in Europe, a new movement called "eugenics" was underway in Nazi Germany. Eugenics advocated for various forms of intervention in the prenatal process in order to improve upon God's creation – perfect it. Eugenics gave rise to selective breeding via prenatal testing, screening, genetic counseling, birth control, in vitro fertilization and genetic engineering. Pandora's Box!

Martin Luther preached dire consequences for going against moral dogma to use contraceptives. The church that bears his name has since totally changed its belief on the topic.

India's Mahatma Gandhi once said: "Moral results can only be produced by moral restraint." Gandhi also preached that using artificial means to contracept was like putting a premium on vice. "Nature is relentless and will have full revenge for any such violation of her laws."

What is nature's intention for fertility?

The mechanics of reproduction

Women normally begin their fertility cycle after reaching puberty, roughly at age twelve. The fertility cycle ends for women around age fifty with the arrival of menopause. Women also will experience a natural period of "extended" infertility while pregnant and under certain circumstances surrounding breastfeeding.

Men, by contrast, gain fertility at puberty and maintain it throughout their lifetime. While previously it was thought that men don't experience menopause, some within the medical community are re-thinking this; they have introduced the concept of a "male menopause," calling it andropause. The symptoms of andropause are not as overt as with menopause (cessation of periods and fertility accompanied by varying degrees of depression, irritability, loss of sex drive, memory loss, and other symptoms) but its affect on a man's ability to become aroused is evident. Research suggests that men in their forties will begin undergoing a 1 percent per year drop in their levels of testosterone.

I caution women and men from drawing comparisons between their mid-life changes. Additionally, even though the medical community offers pharmaceutical-based therapies to offset mid-life symptoms, many of the milder symptoms for both men and women can be addressed by being realistic about external changes, adopting good nutritional habits and living life with a positive attitude. Enjoy the wisdom, stability and experience that are indeed the fruits of aging. As you know, fertility precedes these natural pauses in our life-cycles.

Ovulation is the cyclical eruption of an egg (the female reproductive cell) from the ovary. Several hormones are responsible for this process. Once an egg emerges from its ovary, it begins a five-to-nine-day journey through the fallopian tube with its ultimate destination being the uterus. Should the egg meet and become fertilized by a male sperm (reproductive) cell, life begins. The newly fertilized egg would then continue its journey into the uterus, where the body has made conditions right for it to implant into the uterine lining.

Estrogen is the natural hormone manufactured by the woman's body that is responsible for building up the uterine lining insuring a hospitable environment in which a fertilized egg may implant and fully develop into a viable person. Estrogen also stimulates mucus production; mucus is the substance produced within crypts found in the uterus and its cervix, which is the end of the uterus. Mucus prolongs sperm life and also aids the motility of the sperm; in the absence of mucus, the amount of time that sperm might remain active is dramatically reduced from its typical three- to-five-day window. Estrogen and other key hormones (FSH, LH and progesterone) are responsible for the cyclic ovulations and accompanying menstruation.

If fertilization does not take place during the fertile time in a cycle, the uterine lining sheds one to two weeks later. That process is called menstruation. Dr. Herbert Ratner, a pioneer in natural family planning, referred to menstruation as "a woman's body weeping because a welcome guest failed to arrive."

If fertilization occurs, of course, we have a pregnancy, which is the creation of a new life; new pregnancies can be detected as early as three weeks after the point of conception because a woman will have an elevated temperature pattern. A pregnant woman's temperature will stay elevated for the duration of the pregnancy.

Menstrual irregularity is a common occurrence among teens and young women (older women too). Women in their late twenties and thirties often experience a greater menstrual regularity. Cramping is likely the most frequent complaint among menstruating teens and young women. Young girls who mention such complaints to their physicians might be encouraged to use birth control pills to ease their symptoms.

Parents, please don't encourage your daughters to ingest potent drugs such as birth control pills just to ease menstrual cramps. Real relief is better obtained in other ways. Cramping can be relieved by taking 1,000 milligrams of calcium and 400 milligrams of magnesium before the onset of menstrual bleeding, according to Marilyn Shannon author of *Fertility, Cycles and Nutrition*. Also, an over-the-counter anti-inflammatory pain killer (such as ibuprofen) will offer relief.

There's mounting evidence that despite their wide acceptance and use, oral contraceptives are not safe. The possible side effects are significant but the most frightening are the studies that indicate oral contraceptive use will increase a woman's risk of breast cancer and cervical cancer. It's also been reported that women taking the pill to regulate their cycles had an increased risk of pituitary adenoma, tumors that occur in the pituitary gland. There are a host of documented severe to nuisance side effects associated with using hormonal birth control pills, shots, patches and implants. These risks are written up in "patient warning" pamphlets available from pharmacies that dispense hormonal birth control products. So, even if your daughter is committed to remaining chaste until marriage, she should avoid ingesting birth control pills as a solution to menstrual-related maladies that can be eased through other means.

How oral contraceptives work

A woman's pituitary gland signals to her ovaries to produce two hormones related to the cyclical release of an egg: a follicle stimulating hormone (FSH) and a lutenizing hormone (LH). The ovary also produces estradiol and progesterone under different circumstances and through different signals from the pituitary gland.

When a woman takes oral contraceptives that are composed of synthetic hormones, estrogen and progestin, the contraceptive fools the pituitary gland into producing less FSH and LH, which are needed for ovulation. In other words, the combination of synthetic hormones in the oral contraceptive suppresses or prevents ovulation.

But that's not all. The contraceptive pill also affects the lining of the uterus by depleting it of glycogen, a sugar, resulting in a decrease in the thickness of the uterine lining. When the uterine lining is decreased, so is the overall blood supply necessary to support a developing fertilized egg. (This is why Pill users have scant menstrual periods. Women not ingesting such hormones typically experience four or more days of menstrual bleeding.)

Another consequence to the synthetic hormones used in oral contraception is a thickening of the cervical mucus, which inhibits sperm motility, thereby preventing a sperm from reaching its destination. The synthetic hormones also prematurely age the cervical crypts whereas pregnancy and delivery rejuvenate them. This premature aging, and other side effects, offer insight into why many women experience difficulty achieving pregnancy after discontinuing hormonal birth control.

Does the use of a progestin cause cancer? The short answer is yes. The long answer is that it depends on the potency of the progestin, whether she experienced pregnancy prior to using the pills and other factors.

Can the use of a progestin cause spontaneous abortion? The short answer to that is also yes. Again, highly potent progestin contraceptive pills have a high rate of breakthrough ovulation, according to research conducted by William's Obstetrics and cited in the book *Breast Cancer: It's Link to Abortion and the Birth Control Pill* by Chris Kahlenborn.[2] Two high progestin contraceptives, Norplant and Depo-Provera may be leading women to experience three to four abortions per year, Kahlenborn reports.

What's more, in four studies of women who've had at least one child by age forty-five, there was "at least a 40 percent increased risk of developing breast cancer for those who took birth control pills prior to their first full term pregnancy or within five years of menarche."[3] (Menarche is when girls first begin to have menstrual cycles.)

Kahlenborn also notes that among women younger than forty-five, there was an increased risk of developing breast cancer if that woman had an abortion early in her reproductive life or before her first full-term pregnancy. That increased risk was 50 percent.

Progestins also have been reported to increase a woman's susceptibility to contracting STDs, including HIV, and are linked to an increased risk of cervical cancer.

A young woman whose doctor tries to subscribe oral contraceptives to treat her acne, menstrual irregularity or cramps should run, not walk, to another doctor!

Through the years, oral contraceptive manufacturers have continually tried to reduce the side effects of these drugs by reducing the levels of hormones used in them.

Ironically, one of the most commonly reported side effects of oral contraceptives is a decreased libido, or sex drive.

The morning after pill which we hear about from time to time is nothing more than a super-high dosage of the same oral contraceptive hormones. The dosage alters the lining of the uterus making it an unfavorable environment for a fertilized egg to implant. Because life begins at conception, any contraception that prevents implantation is to be considered an abortifacient.

Barrier contraceptives such as condoms, meanwhile, are distasteful to most couples; this is why so many turn to hormone therapies to control pregnancy. Permanent contraception, otherwise known as sterilization, is currently the most common form of birth control practiced by couples in America. Sterilization is a drastic action that, in a way, speaks to women's discontent over the continued use of oral contraceptives. (If they're so safe, why not keep taking them?) Sterilization methods are often paid for by health insurance while reversal surgeries typically are not. Sterilization is a significant step for any person to make. It makes this statement about one's body, one's life, one's future: I am totally closed to the idea of co-creating a new life.

Natural family planning is the antidote to all these harmful contraceptives and attitudes that damage relationships between husbands and wives.

The natural beauty of natural family planning

There are three categories or methods of natural family planning (NFP) in practice around the world: the Sympto-thermal method, the Mucus-only (or Ovulation) Method, and the Calendar Rhythm Method. Dave and I teach and support the Sympto-thermal method because it teaches all the primary and some secondary signs related to fertility. While the Mucus-only Method is very effective and works for many couples, I believe it is more effective and more advantageous to teach couples all the signs of fertility and then let them decide what they want to do with the information rather than limit their knowledge and awareness from the outset.

Not all Methods train their teachers and their students the same way nor do they cost the same. Couples need to determine for themselves which NFP method they wish to learn.

The Sympto-thermal Method is taught by the Couple to Couple League, based in Cincinnati, Ohio. In the interest of full disclosure, Dave and I have been a CCL volunteer teaching couple for more than twenty-five years and as I write this book, I serve the organization as chairman of the board.

I urge newly-engaged couples not to delay investigating which natural family planning method might best fit their situation. Engaged couples can begin learning NFP immediately so they can become skilled at identifying the intricacies and delicacies of the woman's individual cycle before they are married and use it successfully to either postpone or achieve pregnancy when married.

Integral to the Sympto-Thermal Method is the charting of symptoms; the chart becomes a valuable tool to help detect physical problems, identify possible infertility issues, space pregnancies and even pinpoint conception!

The Sympto-thermal Method involves recording a woman's basal body temperature with a precise basal thermometer. The method also involves making and recording daily observations of a woman's mucus and cervical changes. These observations and measurements are charted daily to reveal a sympto-thermal "event." That event is ovulation.

Couples apply this knowledge whether they plan to abstain from sex and postpone pregnancy or not impose abstinence and try to achieve pregnancy. Couples *do not* have to seek pregnancy with each cycle. Many circumstances warrant postponing pregnancy in a particular cycle – illness, stress, financial considerations, etc.

There have been many instances in our marriage when months or even years passed between pregnancies, giving us needed time and space; the Sympto-thermal Method worked beautifully for us. When we were able to better handle pregnancy, we did. Couples can also use this knowledge about their fertility to recognize early when pregnancy does occur.

Many couples assume they can achieve pregnancy during their first cycle of trying; it is not unusual for six months or longer to pass without getting pregnant and then suddenly, voila! A baby! God's ways are indeed a mystery.

When couples still have not achieved a pregnancy after nine to twelve months of trying using NFP guidelines, they should seek out competent and moral advice from a physician. Many times the NFP charts reveal clues to why, yet, for other couples, infertility will remain a confounding problem.

Couples must always consider the moral implications of their sexual actions whether it involves postponing or achieving pregnancy. Common infertility solutions attempt to replace the natural with completely unnatural actions as they feed couples' desire for pregnancy. The illicit solutions fail to uphold the dignity of the persons involved — parents and baby — while promoting the end as justifying the means.

A couple can easily determine a baby's conception date and project a delivery date by reviewing the data recorded on the fertility chart.

Charting anomalies, such as short mucus patches help a woman determine if she needs medical intervention. We once encouraged a student who was experiencing an unusual amount of colored mucus discharge to seek medical advice; she did and learned she had a sexually transmitted disease. The knowledge and self-awareness that comes through charting is very good.

Today some argue that one can practice natural family planning purely for biological reasons. This may certainly be true. None of the natural methods of family planning I mention utilize synthetic hormones or contraceptive barriers so they also appeal to people who are convicted to using natural remedies and eating organic foods. However, it seems logical that couples who also understand and embrace the moral reasons to use NFP may appreciate it even more. The more reasons one has to practice virtue, the more likely one remains on the right path. Simply put: implementation of natural family planning that separates the moral from the biological is incomplete. The more knowledge a person has about a subject, the better able they are to make sound decisions.

When couples use natural family planning, many change their attitudes about future pregnancies. At first, a couple may only think about natural family planning as a way to postpone another child; then, after months pass, a yearning for another baby often develops. Natural family planning helps couples put into perspective their reasons for abstinence or hopes for another baby; often selfish motives give way to selflessness and a newfound desire to determine God's plan for their family size.

Dave and I have used natural family planning our entire married life; it has been a valuable tool as we've postponed pregnancy and watched fertility return following breastfeeding. Moreover, natural family planning has helped us grow closer to each other. Our chart has been a friend to us all of our married life. We owe much to the Church who deemed natural family planning important enough to recommend it to us when we were engaged. We are also most grateful to God who built our bodies in such a wondrous and scientific way. The knowledge of natural family planning also has been helpful as we've started conversing with our teens about life and sexuality. Through our practice of natural family planning, we've been able to model to our teens some of the necessary elements of a happy marriage – self-control, self discipline and concern for others . ❦

chapter ten

Challenges of Parenting

It's easy to view ourselves as our children's primary teachers as they waddle around us in diapers or as together we settle into a nightly routine of storytelling. These are the warm fuzzy moments of parenting – the times when it's easy to see the rewards of our patient guidance and constant attention because they arrive as soft hugs and unconditional adoration. It is much more difficult to remain steadfast in the knowledge that teens still need strong parental guidance when they purport to "know everything" and dismiss us as "old fashioned" or "out of touch." But the truth is, even when our teens outwardly reject our counsel – as frequently they will – inwardly they desperately want and need it.

Life for teenagers is increasingly complicated. There will be vibrant and sometimes confusing interactions with the opposite sex. The songs they hear and television shows they watch will lead them to believe that instant gratification is in their best interest. When teens pay even the least bit of attention to the media, they will notice that nearly every advertisement – whether it be for beer, cars, sporting events, movies, television shows, deodorant, shampoo or yogurt – will employ images that are highly sexualized. What's more, peers at school might tempt them to defy still emerging values through defiant, sometimes dangerous behavior. The temptation to conform will be great and these temptations come at a time when their brain simply can't process and interpret information in the most mature way.

As teens reach the cusp of adulthood, their challenges will increase. There will be decisions to make regarding higher education. They will face choices that range from a liberal arts degree, a job, training that focuses on skills, or even a religious calling. Most will have to adapt to college life and possible communal living in a dormitory. Some may venture far from home, away from curfews and the watchful eyes of concerned, loving parents. It can be logistically challenging, but parents need to remain engaged counselors for these older teens as they become young adults.

It can be a mistake to believe that a child attending a Christian and Catholic university will be sheltered from assaults against the faith. While some religious institutions of higher learning may not have strayed as far from their religious roots as others, most should be viewed as secular-like institutions; they offer co-ed dormitories like their public counterparts, don't interfere with students' behaviors, such as drinking, having sex, cohabitating, or attending regular religious worship. Many don't make Sunday Mass widely available. A student of faith may face something more troubling at a religious institution. It's entirely possible a child raised by faithful parents may encounter professors who have veered from the teachings of the church and will tailor their curriculum to mirror their dissent.

Will it be easy for an eighteen-year old girl who's been raised to believe God's will for her is to embrace her femininity to counter a pro-contraception professor teaching feminist viewpoints? Whose voice will emerge the clearest to help this girl sort out the conflicting messages – her professor's, her parents', her pastor's, her peer's, or her own? If she can still turn to her parents for guidance and affirmation on the lessons they've taught throughout her teen years, this girl should be content in the knowledge that only God's plan for her life should be of concern. If it has been her parents who have modeled virtuous behavior in their own marriage throughout her upbringing, it will be her parents' voices that rise above any voice of dissent she may encounter at college.

Most parents do want to pass along their faith and give children the benefit of their wisdom earned over the years from gaining knowledge, experience and some plain old hard knocks. Children deserve comprehensive, value-centered information to help them through the tough topics such as casual sex, sexually transmitted diseases, contraception and abortion.

The movement back to God

During the college years or shortly afterward, our children will likely meet someone to whom they consider suitable for a lifelong marriage commitment. When young adults become engaged, they will need to decide if and how to space their children; no doubt they will be barraged by opinions that hold up artificial birth control as superior to natural family planning. This tide of ill-informed, un-Godly advice will swell up from inside the church as much as it will from outside the church. (Catholics use artificial contraception at the same rate as non-Catholics.)

In this instance as with others, it is parents who need be present to inform, guide and teach. You are the ones who need to point out how marketers objectify the human body in order to generate "product demand." You are the ones who need to encourage your son or daughter to seek out partners who hold similar values. You also are the ones who have defined marriage to your children and whom your children will most likely model their own marriages after. And you are the ones who can effectively encourage your children to stand apart from majority opinion and reject the belief that "everybody" uses contraception. You do this by supporting them, supporting others with similar values, and supporting your Church and its efforts to spread the truth.

There is a positive movement alive within the Catholic Church; many, many young people are defying society's notion that everybody uses contraceptives and embraces casual sex. Instead, they embrace the wisdom of the Church as it teaches us virtue both before and after we marry. The movement is based on theology that argues that we are made in the image and likeness of God; thus we are called to act like Him. Not only does this theology argue against all immorality, each year it convinces more young people to adopt natural family planning as the way to space or postpone pregnancies in marriage. It does this by pointing out the obvious: sex is dignified and special and a reflection of authentic love. Anything else is an act of lust or use of another. This naturally reserves sex for the marital union involving two persons who love one another and who are willing to give of themselves totally – without condition. When one person authentically loves the other, each gives the gift of self totally, as what occurs in marital coitus. Remember, conditional love never works out for long.

Male fertility, which is permanent, is symbolic of the fact that God's love for us is permanent. It also may represent the permanence of a husband's love for his wife. Female fertility, which is cyclical, is linked to renewal. God so loves humanity that he continuously offers us opportunities to choose to love Him and grow in knowledge of Him. Additionally, women carry the seeds of new life within them. God appoints men to fertilize those seeds, to allow for the emergence of new life.

In fertility, God becomes a partner to a husband and wife. He gives them the ability, through their love for each other, to create with Him! Why would anyone ever want to close themselves off to such an opportunity?

As teenagers learn about God and His unceasing love for all mankind, it may be easier for them to reject popular culture's false promise for an easier, consequence-free life through the use of contraceptives. Advise your children not to misuse their God-given gift of fertility as they approach the covenant of marriage. Certainly, natural family planning does require self-mastery. But isn't that something you've been encouraging in them since they were toddlers?

All in God's plan

As I said at the outset of this book, most parents do want to pass along their faith and give children the benefit of their wisdom earned over the years from gaining knowledge, experience and some plain old hard knocks. Children deserve comprehensive, value-centered information to help them through the tough topics such as casual sex, sexually transmitted diseases, contraception and abortion. You can't pretend these challenges to faith don't exist in our world because they do. I've given you all the statistics. Remember, silence is not an effective teacher.

The information I've presented here is merely a resource, a starting point – advice I've culled from nearly thirty years of parenting and almost as many years teaching natural family planning. I understand that it is very difficult for some parents to debunk the myths that permeate our society and attack our children. But the cost of doing nothing is too high. The responsibility for teaching children about their bodies lies with you. When parents back away from these responsibilities, children can quickly buckle under the weight of the false promises and myths around them. The only line of defense your children have to protect them from the profane is you. Trust yourself to be the teacher God calls you to be; let the information flow from your heart. Be sincere.

Try to better understand your whole child: his biology, his psychology, his spiritual needs, and his emotional needs with which God gifted you. Teach this child to respect his or her body and to make appropriate choices that enable them to keep Heaven in sight. Understand that all of us, children and parents alike, have become so acclimated by modern events, technology, and moral dilemmas that often, as a coping mechanism, we tune out, turn off the debate, block out our bloodied senses. When we do this, of course, we miss the opportunity to express shock over the truly shocking events that occur in this world. (We also miss out on the opportunity to be awed by awe-inspiring events.) We miss out on crucial moments to instruct our children, too. We miss teaching moments.

Moral dilemmas are teaching moments for all Christians. Facing them is like taking Advanced Placement American History in high school. By contrast, moral relativism – the idea that anything goes – is much like school recess. Who wouldn't want to spend an hour at recess instead of sitting through a lecture in A. P. American History? It's so much easier to believe that everything is relative – everyone should be free to decide their own path.

But parents who wish to raise their children in the faith (and promised such at their child's baptism) cannot spend their time at play. God expects us to teach our children right from wrong and doing so is hard work. He gives us a moral compass as a guide and it becomes our responsibility to give children the necessary guidance so that eventually, their moral compass will properly develop.

When we teach our children the concept of right and wrong, we should expect to be labeled intolerant - or worse. The name calling comes from the parents out in the schoolyard - the ones who choose a life that resembles recess.

Are people of faith intolerant? No. We who love God and seek to live according to His will are called upon to tolerate a lot from society, not the least of which is the near constant assault on our children. People of faith resist the notion that everything is relative; there are "right" and "wrong" answers to life's tough issues - pornography, divorce, abortion, etc. We rely on our moral compass to know what those right and wrong choices are; when we tune into God, He points us toward the path of righteousness. It's up to us to follow Him with love and obedience.

When we choose not to, it's most often because we fear being labeled intolerant. Nobody likes to be called names. If we whitewash issues out of fear or decide to take a neutral stance on issues that are morally objectionable, our families, our children, and society as a whole suffers. God teaches moral absolutes in order that humans can lead happy, fulfilling lives.

The good news is that the Catholic Church champions the areas of love and respect as it affects the human person. This champion uses language that is understandable in today's modern world; it doesn't give way to relativism or secularism. The lesson begins with the story of Genesis, teaching us that all are made in the image and likeness of God. It ends with the story of the Crucifixion and the Resurrection, demonstrating that sacrificial love is part and parcel of a fulfilling life — our Christian life is always a stumbling block to those who don't believe.

It's teachings were renewed under the influence of the late Pope John Paul II and his *Theology of the Body* treatises. It continues under the watchful guidance of Pope Benedect XVI.

Using *Theology of the Body,* the Church has a way to convince others to live and speak an authentic language of love. These teachings should cause us to pause, listen, and ultimately dedicate ourselves to the vision laid out by the Church. The call to cross the thresholds with hope is compelling and authentic. God encourages all of us everywhere and of every state in life not to be afraid. Walk with courage, parents. Gather your children and prepare them to be godly children who act as they do because they authentically love God, love and respect you, and love and respect themselves. Love your sons and daughters unconditionally and forever; inscribe on them the rightful image of being God's son or daughter by using the workbooks that were designed to accompany this book. Good luck and God bless you and yours. ❦

Endnotes

Chapter 2

[1] Feinstein, Sheryl; *Parenting the Teenage Brain*; (Rowman & Littlefield Education, 2007); p.7

[2] Ibid; p.52

[3] Davis, Leslie; *Clothing and Human Behavior: A Review*; (Family and Consumer Sci ences Research Journal 1984); 12(3):325-339

[4] Tiger, Lionel; *The Decline of Males*; (St. Martin's Griffin 1999): 94-95

[5] Ali, S. Omar; Peynirioglu, Zehra; *Songs and Emotions: Are Lyrics and Melodies Equal Partners?* (Psychology of Music 2006); 34(4):512

[6] Greenfield, Patricia; Bruzzone, Lisa; Koyamatsu, Kristi; Satuloff, Wendy; Nixon, Karey; Brodie, Mollyann; and Kingsdale, David; *What is Rock Music Doing to the Minds of our Youth? A First Experimental Look at the Effects of Rock Music Lyrics and Music Videos* (The Journal of Early Adolescence, 1987); 7(3):326

[7] Ibid, pg. 321

[8] Ward, L. Monique; Hansbrough, Edwina; and Walker, Eboni; *Contributions of Music Video Exposure to Black Adolescents' Gender and Sexual Schemas;* (Journal of Adolescent Research, 2005); 20(2):143-146

[9] Jason, Leonard; Fries, Michael; *Helping Parents Reduce Children's Television Viewing;* (Research on Social Work Practice, 2004) 14(2):121

[10] Ibid, 121

[11] Collins, Rebecca; *Sex on Television and It's Impact on American Youth: Background and Results from the RAND Television and Adolescent Sexuality Study;* (Child and Adolescent Psychiatric Clinics of North America, 2005) 14(3):2

[12] Tynes, Brendesha; *Internet Safety Gone Wild?: Sacrificing the Educational and Psychosocial Benefits of Online Social Environments;* (Journal of Adolescent Research, 2007); 22(6):576

[13] Ybarra, Michele; Mitchell, Kimberly; *Exposure to Internet Pornography among Children and Adolescents: A National Survey;* (CyberPsychology & Behavior, 2007); 10(1):71

[14] Olson, Jeremy, *Regular Family Meals Shown to Deter Eating Disorders in Girls,* (St. Paul Pioneer Press) Jan. 8, 2008.

Chapter 4

[1] Fagan, Ron; *Counseling and Therapy for Couples and Families,* (The Family Journal, Pepperdine University, 2006): 14:326

[2] Feinstein, Sheryl; *Parenting the Teenage Brain*; (Rowman & Littlefield Education, 2007); p.54

[3] Fagan, Ron; *Counseling and Therapy for Couples and Families;* (The Family Journal, Pepperdine University, 2006): 14:326

[4] PATS Teens Report; *Generation Rx: National Study Confirms Abuse of Prescription and over the Counter Drugs;* (http://www.drugfree.org, May 15, 2006):3

[5] American Academy of Child and Adolescent Psychiatry: *Child and Adolescent Mental Illness and Drug Abuse Statistics; (*Resources for Families, http://www.aacap.org. Jan 15, 2008): 3.

[6] Feinstein, Sheryl; *Parenting the Teenage Brain*; (Rowman & Littlefield Education, 2007); p.126

[7]Genuis, Stephen J. M.D., *Managing the Sexually Transmitted Disease Pandemic: A Time for Reevaluation;* (American Journal of Obstetrics and Gynecology, 2004); 03(019) 1

[8] Curtiss, Christina & Weinbach, Robert: *Sexually Transmitted Diseases: Response to a Sexist Problem, (*Affilia, Vol.4, No. 4 Winter 1989): 73

[9] Genuis, Stephen J. MD; Genuis, Shelagh; *Teen Reality Check*; (Winfield House Publishing, 2002): 23

[10] Keller, Mary; von Sadovszky, Victoria; Pankratz, Barbara; Hermsen, Joan; Sowell, Richard; Demi, Alice: *Self Disclosure of HPV Infection to Sexual Partners;* (Western Journal of Nursing Research, 2000): 22:287

[11] Ibid.

Chapter 5

[1] Olson, Jeremy, *Regular Family Meals Shown to Deter Eating Disorders in Girls,* (St. Paul Pioneer Press) Jan. 8, 2008.

[2] http://www.4girls.gov/nutrition/weight.htm

Chapter 6

[1] U.S. Centers for Disease Control, *Abortion Surveillance — U.S.*, 1998; (MMWR, 2002): 51 (SS03): 1-32

[2] Kasun, Jacqueline; *The War Against Population;* (Ignatius Press 1988): 149

[3] http://www.johnstonsarchive.net/policy/abortion/ab-unitedstates.html, updated 6-4-2008.

[4] *Abortion Statistics by U.S. State, Age, Race and Worldwide Statistics;* http://www.abortiontv.com/misc/abortionstatistics.htm
[5] Sproul, R.C.; *Abortion*; (Navpress, 1990): 132-133
[6] Ibid; 133
[7] Public Health News; *Rape Case Incidence Down In U.S., Statistics Show;* (http://www.medicalnewstoday.com/medicalnews.php?newsid=45481); *June 21, 2006.*
[8] Roberts, Sam; *Who We Are Now;* (Henry Holt & Co., 2004): 34
[9] Ibid; 184
[10] Ibid; 34

Chapter 8

[1] Rose, Michael; *Goodbye, Good Men*; (Regnery Publishing Inc., 2002): 48
[2] http://www.priestsofdarkness.com/stats.html.

Chapter 9

[1] Blue Cross and Blue Shield Health Publication: *The Maturing Male and Menopause: Fact or fiction? Fallacy or Fantasy?* Winter 2005; 14(4):1
[2] Kahlenborn, Chris; *Breast Cancer: It's Link to Abortion and the Birth Control Pill:* (One More Soul, 2002): 198
[3] Ibid; 137

Bibliography

A Consumer's Guide to the Pill and Other Drugs by John Wilks; TGB Books (1996)

Abortion by R.C. Sproul; Navpress (1990)

Breast Cancer: Its Link to Abortion and the Birth Control Pill by Chris Kahlenborn; One More Soul (2000)

Brave New Family by G.K. Chesterton; Edited by Alvaro de Silva; Ignatius Press (1990)

Catholicism and Fundamentalism by Karl Keating; Ignatius Press (1988)

Decline of Males by Lionel Tiger; St. Martin Grinnin (1999)

Fertility Cycles and Nutrition by Marilyn Shannon; The Couple to Couple League International (1996)

Fighting for Your Marriage by Howard Markman, Scott Stanely, and Susan Blumberg; Jossey-Bass Inc Publishers (1994)

G.K. Chesterton: The Apostle of Common Sense by Dale Ahlquist; Ignatius Press (2003)

Humanae Vitae: A Generation Later by Janet Smith; Catholic University of America Press (1991)

Is NFP Good? by Reverends Richard Hogan and John LeVoir; The Couple to Couple League International (2005)

Life Matters by A. Roger and Rebecca Merrill; McGraw Hill (2003)

Loving Your Marriage Enough to Protect It by Jerry Jenkins; Moody Press (1993)

Magnificat Monthly

Mother Angelica's Answers, Not Promises by Mother Angelica with Christine Allison; Harper Row (1987)

Natural Family Planning; DeRance Inc (1980)

Nothing But the Truth by Karl Keating ; Catholic Answers (1999)

Parenting the Teenage Brain by Sheryl Feinstein; Rowman and Littlefield (2007)

Pornified by Pamela Paul; Henry Holt & Co. (2005)

Raising Them Chaste by Richard and Renee Durfield; Bethany House Publishers (1991)

Sexual Chemistry by Ellen Grant, M.D.; Mandarin Paperbacks (1994)

Sexuality and Sexually Transmitted Diseases by Joe McIlhaney, Jr.; Baker Book House Publishing (1990)

Smart Sex by Jennifer Roback Morse; Spence Publishing Co. (2005)

Sterilization Reversal by John Long; One More Soul (2003)

Teen Sex Reality Check by Stephen Genuis, M.D., and Shelagh Genuis; Winfield House Publishing (2002)

The Art of Natural Family Planning; The Couple to Couple League International (2007)

The Battle for the Catholic Mind edited by William May and Kenneth Whitehead; Fellowship of Catholic Scholars (2001)

The Cost of Choice edited by Erika Bachiochi; Encounter Books (2004)

The Decline and Fall of the Catholic Church in America by David Carlin; Sophia Institute Press (2003)

The Hidden Pope by Darcy O'Brien; Daybreak Books (1998)

The O'Reilly Factor for Kids by Bill O'Reilly; Harper (2004)

The Way We Never Were by Stephanie Coontz; Perseus Book Group (1992)

United States History from 1865 by Arnold Rice and John Krout; American Book-Works Corporation (1991)

Who We Are Now by Sam Roberts; Henry Holt and Co. (2004)

Young and Catholic by Tim Drake; Sophia Institute Press (2004)

INDEX

W

Y

Z